THE MINGLING OF SOULS

THE MINGLING OF SOULS

GOD'S DESIGN FOR LOVE, MARRIAGE, SEX & REDEMPTION

MATT CHANDLER

WITH JARED C. WILSON

David C Cook
transforming lives together

THE MINGLING OF SOULS
Published by David C Cook
4050 Lee Vance View
Colorado Springs, CO 80918 U.S.A.

David C Cook Distribution Canada
55 Woodslee Avenue, Paris, Ontario, Canada N3L 3E5

David C Cook U.K., Kingsway Communications
Eastbourne, East Sussex BN23 6NT, England

The graphic circle C logo is a registered trademark of David C Cook.

The website addresses recommended throughout this book are offered as a
resource to you. These websites are not intended in any way to be or imply an
endorsement on the part of David C Cook, nor do we vouch for their content.

Scripture quotations marked ESV are taken from The Holy Bible, English Standard
Version® (ESV®), copyright © 2001 by Crossway, a publishing ministry of Good
News Publishers. Used by permission. All rights reserved; NET are taken from
the NET Bible® copyright © 1996–2006 by Biblical Studies Press, L.L.C. http://
netbible.com. All rights reserved; NIV are taken from the Holy Bible, New
International Version®, NIV®. Copyright © 1973, 2011 by Biblica, Inc.™ Used by
permission of Zondervan. All rights reserved worldwide. www.zondervan.com.
The author has added italics to Scripture quotations for emphasis.

LCCN 2014948797
ISBN 978-1-4347-0686-7
eISBN 978-0-7814-1282-7

The Team: Andrew Stoddard, Amy Konyndyk, Nick Lee,
Carly Razo, Helen Macdonald, Karen Athen
Cover Design: Eric Bowman
Cover Photo: Amanda Jameson

Printed in the United States of America
First Edition 2015

3 4 5 6 7 8 9 10

081215

Lauren: What a gift you are to me. I am not wise or clever enough with words to adequately explain all that God has given me in you!

CONTENTS

ACKNOWLEDGMENTS   9

INTRODUCTION   11

1   ATTRACTION   21

2   DATING   49

3   COURTSHIP: AN OLD IDEA REVIVED   71

4   WEDDING BELLS   97

5   "AND THE TWO BECOME ONE FLESH"   119

6   FIGHTING FAIR   143

7   LOGS ON THE FIRE   177

8   "I'M NOT GOING ANYWHERE"   195

CONCLUSION   217

NOTES   219

ACKNOWLEDGMENTS

I first heard Tommy Nelson teach through the Song of Songs in 2002. I had been married only a couple of years, and I devoured those CDs like a thirsty man in the desert. I listened to most of them multiple times, and his teachings left an indelible mark on the way I understand this important book.

In the thirteen years since, I have studied the Song of Songs enough times to know that Tommy's interpretation is in keeping with historical scholarly consensus. The Song of Songs charts the relationship between a woman and King Solomon from the initial attraction through the marital consummation to the place of keeping the flame of romance burning after familiarity has set in. I am still grateful for Tommy's inspiring passion for the Song of Songs—without it, you probably wouldn't be holding *The Mingling of Souls* in your hands.

Additionally, this book wouldn't exist without the countless number of men and women at The Village Church who have sought my counsel and the wisdom found in the Scriptures on dating, courtship, marriage, and intimacy. I have returned again and again to Solomon's Song on multiple occasions when counseling married couples who as they have grown older have sought to navigate the challenge of growing more deeply and more passionately in love.

Last but certainly not least, without the patience, grace, and godliness of my wife, Lauren, this book surely wouldn't be in your hands. Her steadfastness through the first seven years of our marriage—which were extremely difficult—has, by God's grace, given birth to the depth, beauty, and passion of the last eight years.

INTRODUCTION

When I began writing this book, Amazon.com listed for sale 151,000 books on marriage; 27,000 books on dating; almost 12,000 books on attraction; and more than 190,000 books on sex. On the page listing books on the subject of marriage, the "sponsored links" suggested pages on topics such as "aggressive divorce" and "divorce help for women," among others. Clearly, we are a culture simultaneously obsessed with relationships and sex, but dysfunctional in our approaches to them.

In the church I pastor, I am continually bombarded with questions about how dating should work, and we spend thousands of hours a year in premarital and marital counseling. Although there appears to be a deep desire to approach dating, marriage, and sex in a way that pleases God, there nevertheless seems to be a profound lack of wisdom and practical know-how. There is a sizable gap between our understanding of the gospel and our knowledge of the Scriptures on one hand and our application of that knowledge on the other. The sheer amount of confusion, heartbreak, and fear that I have witnessed at The Village Church in regard to romantic relationships and sex provides my primary motivation for writing this book.

But it is not enough to continually restate the problems. Christian culture does not lack for well-meaning hand-wringing in the areas of sexual morality, and the unbelieving world is not necessarily unclear on where the church stands in these areas either. It is also not enough to simply offer practical help on the topics of communication, romance, and sexuality. Practical help is—well, *helpful*—and I want to share some wisdom in those areas with you. But practical steps take us only so far without the right motivations and the right character. Any truly biblical treatment of these subjects must go deeper than outward application. The Holy Spirit is first dedicated to our inward transformation. And the good news is that God is committed to this work.

Yes, there is good news amid all the confusion surrounding romance, marriage, and sex. And it's actually found in the first sentence of the Bible: "In the beginning, God created the heavens and the earth."[1] That simple yet profound sentence gives us the authoritative lens through which to see the world. The universe that you and I inhabit was created and ordered and is sovereignly governed by a good Creator-God. One of the implications of this truth is that there is now wisdom woven into the very fabric of life that, if submitted to, makes life "to the full" possible.[2]

But submission to this wisdom doesn't come easily. Two chapters into the book of Genesis, we see sin's arrival wreaking havoc on the creative order, poisoning every earthly relationship—beginning with Adam's marriage to Eve. Where the relationship between man and woman was originally one of joyful exuberance and complementarity, sin made it confusing, fraught with conflict, and at times extremely painful.

This is not the way God designed the world to run. And yet, a mistake Christians often make is confusing the perversion for the design. We see all the pain and anxiety that result from relationships in conflict, particularly in the areas of sex and sexuality, and we begin to treat sex and the desire for it as bad in and of themselves. But the ways we abuse a thing do not negate the value of that thing. Misuse does not disprove the proper use. So when the Scriptures say that God scooped the dirt up from the ground and shaped man, we acknowledge that this means *all* of him. I'm not trying to be crass here, but when God shaped the man, he gave the man a penis. It wasn't the Devil who did that. God didn't mold most of the man and then let Satan add his own touch. Neither did Satan sneak in and alter God's good creation.

No, for whatever power the Devil has, he is still not a creator; he just perverts and twists God's good designs. God put the penis on the man, and he put the testicles on the man, and he filled those testicles with sperm. He created all tissue—some that would expand, some that would secrete; he filled the man with testosterone that would drive much of his life. From the beginning, this was God's idea. Then he sent the man out filled with testosterone to walk through all creation and name the animals, to exercise God-given authority. When Adam was done with that, before sin entered the world, God said, "It is not good that the man should be alone; I will make him a helper fit for him."[3]

I want to say it again: God's the one who created and wired this whole thing. In Genesis 2, sin hadn't even entered the world yet, and God said it wasn't good for Adam to be alone. So he knocked him out, pulled out a rib, and shaped the woman. And as he shaped the woman differently, he gave her larger breasts, rounder hips, and a vagina. He filled the woman with a different hormone, estrogen. The woman's body was not the Devil's idea; it was all God's doing.

When Adam woke up, he looked at the woman, and the whole literary form shifted. He began to sing. Adam had been naming the animals—camel, donkey, horse, fish—and then he broke into song when he saw the woman. "This at last," his song began, as if he had been longing for some undefined fulfillment all along. After all, there had been no helper found suitable for him among the animal world. But this creature? "At last!"

He named her *woman*, which from the Hebrew essentially means "out of me" or "mine." How profound is that? After he named all the animals, he sang the first love song the moment he laid eyes on Eve. He sang, "Mine." This is itself a foretaste of the declaration in the Song of Solomon, "My beloved is mine, and I am his."[4]

As Genesis 2 closes, we see God's plan for relationships and sex. He says that the man and the woman "were both naked and were not ashamed."[5] Think for a minute about that verse, and especially the phrase "naked and … not ashamed." It's clear in the text that they are physically naked, but it is also clear that the relationship Adam and Eve have—the one that is God's good design for us—is that of a man and a woman serving the Lord together, with nothing to fear and nothing to hide, with everything to be glad about in God, including this good gift of each for the other in the covenant of marriage.

God also commanded the man and the woman to "be fruitful and multiply."[6] God gave them the gift of sex. In the physical body, sexual intercourse wasn't some random happening. No, this, too, was God's gift. "Be fruitful and multiply; enjoy one another."

Sex and the families it produces are part of God's blessing. From the initial attraction to the covenant marriage that sanctions sex, from the thrill of the romantic chase to the consummate pleasure of the marriage bed, God designed it all, ordered it all, blessed it all.

It is imperative that you understand this important point before we get too far into this book. It is necessary, for the understanding of all God has made, to know that God *intentionally* made the universe in a way that brings him great glory and us great joy.

God's good design when it comes to gender and relationships and sex is for all of these things to work rhythmically together in such a way that men and women experience the deepest amount of joy possible while at the same time glorifying God at the highest level possible. The longing in a single person's heart for a wife or a husband finds its root in God's glory.

Wouldn't it be nice if it still worked the way it did in Genesis? Men, if you got up from a nap and there she was! No games, no confusion, no risk. Just "the one" standing before you, glowing with God's delight. Women, can you wrap your minds around a relationship built on clarity and trust, all for your joy and God's glory? No broken hearts, no mind games, no toying with your emotions. Just serving the Lord with a man who delights in God all the more because God gave him *you*. What a stunning dynamic God's relational order would create! This is what Adam and Eve enjoyed. Pure, uninhibited, harmonious, glory-filled rapture with each other through pure, uninhibited, harmonious, glory-filled relationship with God.

So what happened? Well, Genesis 3 happened. We discover there that sin entered the world through Adam's and Eve's disobedience, fracturing the harmony and disrupting and disgracing the rhythm. Think of a really loud electric guitar that's not playing correctly in a band. It's discordant and distracting. You can sort of sense how the song was *meant* to be played, but the dissonance is obscuring the beauty, the harmony. The guitarist might not even know he's off.

Similarly, sometimes we are pursuing God's good gifts in ways he has not designed them to be pursued, outside the bounds of the glory of his righteousness. We may think we are joining in a beautiful song, but we are actually contributing to the disharmony of the fallen world. A gift that is beautiful, good, perfect, and purposed for our joy may instead begin to harm us (if not kill us) while we try to enjoy the residual good in it.

I'll give you some examples.

Wine, which the Scriptures say is from the Lord and for people to enjoy, eventually can give way to alcoholism when pursued for its own sake. Food, which is from the Lord and given to humanity for both sustenance and enjoyment, becomes gluttony when pursued self-centeredly. Every good gift God gives us, in fact, becomes an idol when we pursue it for its own sake and for our ultimate pleasure and glory. This is true of good gifts, such as family and children and even church. And it is certainly true of gifts designed to facilitate pleasure, such as food and drink and sex. When sin entered the world, what was meant to lead people to the worship of God became something with the potential to harm.

Sex is a gift from God. It is meant to nurture intimacy in a marriage and forge a bonding of souls. Unfortunately, sex in our culture has become almost exclusively a physical thing. We've made the word *love* a junk-drawer word. It's the word that means everything. People will say they "love" their children but also that they "love" their dogs. Surely they don't mean the same thing. A husband who "loves" his wife but also "loves" his favorite NFL team isn't saying the same thing.

In the Hebrew lexicon, there are multiple words for *love*, but one of my favorites is the word *dod*. Although it is often rendered "love," *dod* refers specifically to sexual love and is better translated as "lovemaking" or "caresses." It carries the meaning, as Paul House said, of two souls mingling together.[7]

God's plan is for a man and a woman in the bond of the marriage covenant to have their souls—not just their bodies—become one.

Sounds amazing, doesn't it? A mingling of souls. I want to know how we get there, don't you?

The source of that kind of joy and fulfillment is the same source for all sin's remedy. If we backtrack to the reason we got into all this mess, we can connect the dots to see God's promise of the way out. The reason we struggle in relationships, marriage, and sex is because we are sinners. Therefore, the antidote for our sin must be the antidote for our struggles.

Relationships, sex, and intimacy are God's ideas, and even though our selfish rebellion fractured God's good design, God reconciled everything back to himself through the life, death, and resurrection of his Son, Jesus Christ. This includes sex and relationships! Our gracious God has not left us in the dark.

Right there in the middle of the Bible, he inspired five books we have traditionally called "the Wisdom Books"—Job, Psalms, Proverbs, Ecclesiastes, and the Song of Songs. These books of divine wisdom reveal to us in song and poetry and dialogue the Lord's beautiful ways of living and dying and everything in between. And in that fifth Wisdom Book, the Song of Songs (or the Song of Solomon), we watch a couple navigate the age-old pursuit of romance—the pursuit, actually, of one another—as they fight for purity against their flesh, embrace the gracious covenant of marriage, celebrate the amazing gift of sex, and learn how to gracefully grow old together. All the

while they disagree honorably, encourage constantly, and keep the
fires of a godly romance burning.

The bride and her groom do all of this in a way that gives God
glory and brings themselves great joy and deep intimacy. We would
do well to watch and imitate them. Now, I don't think the Song is a
Christian guide to dating. I don't really think there is such a thing.
Charles Spurgeon, the "Prince of Preachers," did say this about the
Song of Songs:

> This Book stands like the tree of life in the midst of
> the garden, and no man shall ever be able to pluck
> its fruit, and eat thereof, until first he has been
> brought by Christ past the sword of the cherubim,
> and led to rejoice in the love which hath delivered
> him from death. The Song of Solomon is only to
> be comprehended by the men whose standing is
> within the veil. The outer-court worshippers, and
> even those who only enter the court of the priests,
> think the Book a very strange one; but they who
> come very near to Christ can often see in this Song
> of Solomon the only expression which their love to
> their Lord desires.[8]

Spurgeon was saying that only those aware of the steadfast love
of God found in Christ could fully understand the type of ferociously
committed love we see in the Song. So, again, although this is no
Christian dating guide, it is clear from the book that there is a wise
way to approach the opposite sex and that there is a foolish way. What

we see in the Song is saturated with wisdom, and the believer in Christ will be reminded of the nurturing, patient, steadfast love of our Savior.

A quick confession: I have been with my wife, Lauren, for seventeen years. We dated for a year, courted for six months, were engaged for another six months, and have been married for fifteen years. Unfortunately, Lauren and I didn't follow quite a bit of what we're about to walk through in this book. You might think this makes me a hypocrite, that what I wrote isn't worth the paper it's printed on. But I would argue that this hard-learned reality actually makes me *more* confident in what I am writing. We have personally experienced some of the heartbreak, confusion, and frustration that result from going with the flow of modern relational dynamics.

I am aware of the multiple ways I failed to lead us as a couple. But I'm also aware—vividly so—of how God's merciful gospel redeemed many of the foolish decisions we made and brought incredible healing to our hearts. But I pray that you will not presume upon the Lord and do whatever you want because you believe he will "fix it all" by his grace in the future. Grace does not make sin safe.

Grace does make *sinners* safe. The grace of God in Jesus Christ, the sinless Bridegroom who laid down his life for the church in order to present her as blameless to the Father in great glory, so secures the children of God who make up this bride that they need not fear, as Luther said, "sinning boldly." Luther wasn't encouraging us to walk in ways that are contrary to the commands of God. Rather, he was reminding us that regardless of whatever perversions we are guilty of, God's grace covers that perversion, and we are encouraged to run to him and not from him. We can come just as we are to Jesus Christ; he does not love some future version of us, but he loves the real us, the wounded us, the messy us, the broken us. And what we learn in the Song of Songs is that a marriage shaped according to this gospel of grace, forged over years of hard-earned trust and forgiveness, can be an unsafe place for sin but a very safe place for sinners.

In a gospel-centered marriage, when two souls are mingled together with the Holy Spirit's leading, we find confirmation after confirmation that grace is true, that grace is *real*—that we can be really, truly, deeply known and at the same time really, truly, deeply loved.

CHAPTER ONE

ATTRACTION

If you watch little boys and girls from birth to around age two, they are rarely aware of each other's differences. But gradually they begin to notice their unique distinctions, and by preschool or kindergarten, they are keenly aware that they are different. Around this time, children tend to split off and hang out with their own sex. They will occasionally shove one another or argue, but for most, the preference is to run with their own kind.

Most boys like to wrestle and climb, and they like to build and then destroy whatever it is they built. This behavior is of course unacceptable to the majority of little girls who play more relationally. I have two daughters, and both of them when they were this age would make any two objects friends. A pencil and a spoon would have conversation and laugh together. The friendship between the pencil and the spoon wouldn't last long in the world of boys where destruction is always imminent. Mr. Pencil's leaden guts would be spilling out, and Mr. Spoon would be laughing his silver face off.

As boys and girls get a bit older, they begin to mingle a little more but still stay predominantly with their own kind. The first bit of flirtation will be disguised as dislike. When boys playfully begin picking on girls (and vice versa), it is usually a kind of first "Hey, something is changing here" moment. The teasing and pranking are basically fourth-grade-ese for "I have weird feelings for you but don't know what to do with them."

And then it happens: Somewhere between fifth and ninth grades, depending on a variety of factors affecting development and awareness, what I like to call the "Day of Epiphany" occurs. Up until this moment, a child has been largely indifferent to the opposite sex or even thought they were "gross." But on the Day of Epiphany, something changes.

Do you remember that day? You woke up that morning for school, got dressed, put on your shoes, slung your backpack over your shoulder, saw your friends, and then as you were walking toward your crew, you saw him or her, and all of a sudden he or she wasn't gross anymore. The indifference and repulsion had vanished. A particular member of the opposite sex caught your eye in a suddenly different way, and, well … you kind of *wanted* one. This is the Day of Epiphany.

I served in youth ministry for a decade, and I witnessed firsthand the marked change between most sixth graders and ninth graders. For instance, if you gather together one hundred sixth graders for three days, by the end of that third day, the environment will smell like body odor and cheap cologne. But by the time they hit ninth grade, the boys are taking showers and styling their hair. All of a sudden they care about the kind of clothes they're wearing, how they look, and how they smell. What happened to those funky-smelling sixth-grade boys? The Day of Epiphany.

What seemed to matter very little before now matters *immensely*. Boys in ninth grade now care very much what ninth-grade girls think about them. Boys go from wanting to appear repulsive to wanting to appear impressive, especially to girls. The Day of Epiphany changes everything. After the Day of Epiphany, boys begin to pursue and girls begin to want to be pursued.

There are certainly exceptions to everything I've outlined above, but by and large, this smelling and teasing, wooing and pursuing is the typical trajectory through the onset of puberty for boys and girls. And the important thing to remember is this: it is all by God's good design.

ATTRACTION

Attraction is a strange, ambiguous force. The *Psychology Dictionary* defines *attraction* as "the natural feeling of being drawn to other individuals and desiring their company. This is usually (but not necessarily) due to having a personal liking for them."[1] That's a little vague, but then again, so is attraction. We feel ourselves drawn to people, whether romantically or not, because they have "a certain something." It's usually not just one thing, but a variety of characteristics or impressions, that attracts us to one another. There are lots of beautiful people in the world, of course, but most of us feel drawn romantically to members of the opposite sex we find physically attractive *plus something else*.

And yet, when it comes to romance, there is something physical that typically draws us to someone else. When we say we find someone "attractive" today, this is basically what we mean: we find that person physically appealing. He or she is good-looking. For both men and women, but especially for men, our initial attraction may have little to do with the person's character or competency but rather emerges simply from liking the way he or she looks. This is only logical, because physical appearance is the first thing we notice, and it takes a while longer to get to know someone's character. For the moment, we look across a room and see someone who is physically appealing.

It ought to go without saying, but it doesn't, so I'll say it: There is nothing wrong with this process of being physically attracted to someone. It's completely natural. In fact, the Song of Songs begins this way: "Let him kiss me with the kisses of his mouth! For your love is better than wine" (1:2). The woman in the Song saw Solomon, and she liked what she saw. She wanted him to kiss her, and just looking at him made her glad. He was what we might call "eye candy."

Over and over, in fact, the Bible doesn't just describe physical attraction between the sexes; it *sanctions* it. From Adam's love-at-first-sight song about Eve in Genesis 2 to Jacob's immediate attraction to Rachel in Genesis 29, where verse 17 tells us she was "beautiful in form and appearance," we do not see the Scriptures opposed to physical attraction. Certainly, the Bible's wisdom on God's design for romance is more than physical attraction, but it's not less than that. Nor is it even something we are advised to outgrow. Even as your love for your spouse deepens and takes on the character of more thorough knowledge of your spouse's weaknesses, wounds, and sins, the instruction to pursue physical attraction throughout the years remains. Thus, the father advised his young son in Proverbs 5:19 about his wife: "Let her breasts fill you at all times with delight; be intoxicated always in her love." Note the word "always."

Nearly all of us will always be physically attracted to what we consider beautiful. Our tastes and interests might vary, but the instinct itself is fairly common across the billions of human beings in the world: we are attracted to those we find possessing of beauty. Beauty is that particular combination of qualities that especially pleases the sight. It is, as the saying goes, "in the eye of the beholder." Men find beautiful a woman's particular shape (curvy or thin, according to taste) or style of hair or dress, and women may find beautiful a man's particular eye color (blue or brown) or physique (toned or burly). We naturally notice these qualities across a room, and even if just mentally, we are drawn to the people we find "beautiful."

The fact that we all tend to have different tastes when it comes to physical attraction proves how creative and versatile our Creator's artistry truly is. And the fact that we all tend to find *somebody* physically attractive proves how brilliantly our Creator has embedded in us the very appreciation of beauty (which is to say, more deeply, the appreciation of *glory*, of which his own is the pinnacle). The natural *and biblical* reality is that most human beings are going to be physically attracted to the opposite sex. This is a good and right thing. But according to the same Word of God that sanctions physical attraction, we must be very careful with it.

BEAUTY IS VAIN

As I've noted, the Bible has much to say about physical beauty. But we should expect that God's Word on beauty is not as one-dimensional as our own. Although the very reality of beauty presupposes the nature of attraction, we also see that beauty, according to the wisdom of God, can be deceptive.

For example, in the book of Proverbs, there are warnings given to the male reader about being unduly captivated by a woman's beauty. In Proverbs 6:25, we read the caution, "Do not desire her beauty in your heart, and do not let her capture you with her eyelashes." Is the Lord speaking out of both sides of his mouth? Are we supposed to be attracted to a woman physically but at the same time *not?*

In a way, yes. The key phrase related to desire in Proverbs 6:25 is "in your heart," with the added helpful context of the word "capture." This is not the same as being "captivated," which can be a good thing. What the Bible repeatedly challenges us toward is getting beyond mere external appearances and wisely considering beauty of the heart.

Another well-known biblical warning is found in Proverbs 31:30: "Charm is deceitful, and beauty is vain, but a woman who fears the LORD is to be praised." For beauty to be vain means it can be superficial—preoccupied solely with the external. For beauty to be deceitful means it can trick us into missing a deeper, darker reality. We can be mistaken by the lure of beauty into being captured— namely, by sin.

In the Bible we see a reflection of a pervasive cultural recognition: it is very often the more physically attractive who prove to be more spiritually deceptive. We can be easily baited by our attractions down the wrong paths. In Matthew 23:27–28, Jesus admonished the Pharisees for their superficially religious behavior:

> Woe to you, scribes and Pharisees, hypocrites! For you are like whitewashed tombs, which outwardly appear beautiful, but within are full of dead people's bones and all uncleanness. So you also outwardly appear righteous to others, but within you are full of hypocrisy and lawlessness.

The old saying that "beauty is only skin-deep" is rich with biblical truth. It is true of the attractive harlot in Proverbs. It is true of David's sinful pursuit of Bathsheba. It is true of Samson's lurid relationship with Delilah. And it is certainly true of the deceptive schemes of the evil one himself, whom we are told often masquerades as "an angel of light" (2 Cor. 11:14).

This is not to say, of course, that you ought to marry somebody you find unattractive! It means only that our romance—sense of beauty itself—must run much deeper than physical attraction. Certainly in marriage, the ongoing nurturing of attraction must endure the changes that come with the years, affected by the bearing of children, the slowing of metabolisms, the weathering of skin, and even the ravages of illness and hardship. Romance in marriage, for it to be truly a mingling of souls, cannot simply be a mingling of body parts. No, we must acknowledge both the blessing and the danger of beauty.

THE EVOLVING IDEAL

Another reason we must be careful with the concept of physical attraction is because of how arbitrary it can be. Tastes vary person to person. But they also vary culture to culture and age to age. Indeed, attraction that is rooted simply in the physical is culturally determined and changes depending on where you are in the world and where you are in history. We are all subject to the evolving ideal of beauty, which Reischer and Koo outline in detail in their article "The Body Beautiful."[2]

My sister and her husband have lived in Asia for close to eight years. Whenever I visit, I notice the ideal for beauty is different there from where I live in Texas. For instance, women in Asia seemingly desire light skin; the stores there proliferate with creams and lotions that will help women bleach their skin to increasingly whiter shades. I must have seen twenty commercials for these products and another hundred or so billboards. In the Dallas area, the opposite is true. Women long for the summer months when they can lie by the pool and soak up the sun's rays, transforming their white, wintery skin by roasting it, basically, until their flesh resembles that of a bronzed goddess. This is just one of hundreds of cultural examples of different beauty standards around the world. Which culture is right? Is bleached or tanned skin more beautiful?

When we look at the vast trajectory of history, the cultural landscape gets even more complex. The "ideal woman" throughout the ages has morphed over and over again, sometimes quite dramatically.[3] From more ancient times through the Middle Ages, in European cultures especially, women with pale skin and more shapely figures were considered exceptionally beautiful. When we look at paintings of beautiful women from these time periods, we may think they look fat and unattractive. And yet what passes for "hot" in today's culture would have been considered sickly back then. In the early twentieth century (especially in the 1920s), women cut their hair very short into "bobs" and wore dresses to conceal their figures. In the 1940s, the introduction of tan skin and longer, flowing hair became the standard of beauty.

And on and on the ever-changing standard goes.

Today there seems to be a hodgepodge of styles that cover the full range of history in defining "beauty." Perhaps one of the best examples is the popular Barbie. One researcher provides a summary:

> Even our toys are undergoing "the knife" in the name of beauty. In 1997, Mattel's most famous toy, the Barbie doll, emerged from the factory operating room with a "wider waist, slimmer hips, and ... a reduction of her legendary bustline" (*Wall Street Journal* 1997). This reconfiguration of the West's premiere icon of femininity after nearly forty years suggests that the image of femininity embodied by the original Barbie of the late 1950s has undergone a radical transformation of its own. Beauty, though highly subjective, is more than simply a matter of aesthetics or taste. Cultural ideals of beauty are also an index and expression of social values and beliefs—so much so that "the history of [society] is in large measure the history of women's beauty" (Jury & Jury 1986).[4]

Feminists lament what they call the oppressive "male gaze" that has objectified the female form since the beginning of time, and they are not entirely off the mark. The idea is that feminine beauty exists for male pleasure and is in fact determined by male pleasure. Generation to generation, it seems, the incessant but unstable feminine ideal, driven largely by males, has shaped the very generations themselves. Can there be any doubt that especially in our advertising age, sex sells, and that this superficial commoditizing of beauty and sex has made us both a more visual culture while also a more vulnerable one? Aren't we simply objectifying each other to dullness?

Our understanding of beauty in relation to men has not evolved the same way it has for women. Making the comparison between the Renaissance and today, the idea of what is considered physically attractive has not changed all that much for men. Men have been and are still considered attractive based generally on their height and the broadness of their shoulders.

The more recent struggle for men is the evaluation of "true masculinity." There is a growing crisis about the meaning of masculinity itself, a crisis that points to the betrayal of men by the very hypermasculine ideals that they are meant to embody. On the one hand, coming out of the hippie movement of the sixties and seventies, men were expected to become more sensitive, more "in touch with their feminine side." Then there seemed to be a revolt against this perceived effeminacy in the late seventies and early eighties with the rise of the free-swingin', macho types and the rise of crass jock culture.

Ideals for men have vacillated back and forth ever since, as the eighties and nineties gave us the sensitive grunge rockers and the sex-hungry party boys. From the beginning of the twenty-first century onward, we have seen the rise of "metrosexuals," the protohipster males, and now we seem to be witnessing a revival of the swaggering alpha males with their beers and beards. Is it any surprise that in the dizzying lust of the broken male perspective toward women we wouldn't become confused about what it means to be a man? Should we be sensitive or tough? If both, when? How do we display sensitivity in a way that doesn't make us effeminate? And how do we display toughness in a way that doesn't make us chauvinistic or stubborn?

This pervasive cultural gender confusion has complicated the so-called ideal of beauty for both men and women and turned us all into a confused mess.

THE REAL YOU IS THE INNER YOU

We've established that the force that grabs our attention and pulls us like a tractor beam into relationships is more than likely physical attraction. And we've established that this is not a bad thing; we simply must take great care to not let it drive us into relationships that are toxic and ungodly (or drive toxic and ungodly ideas into our relationships).

I recently sat down with a non-Christian who attends our church. He wanted to discuss some of his doubts about the things we teach and to ask me pointed questions. By all physical indicators he would be a good catch. He is in his midtwenties, single, handsome, attends church regularly, and is quite wealthy. During our conversation he told me that one of the reasons he attends our church is because the type of woman he wants to marry can't be found in the clubs he frequents. He wants to marry a church girl.

Here I am sitting in a room with a guy who goes out on the weekends to "hook up" with women, then gets up, showers, and comes to our church to look for a young woman to marry. I felt my heart getting angrier and angrier the more we talked, and I informed him that he couldn't hunt at The Village. The world is filled with men and women who have a veneer of relational health and godliness but underneath are driven by selfishness, lust, and the need for control. That's why the second line of dialogue in the Song of Songs is so important. The woman liked looking at Solomon, but she knew something else too: "Your anointing oils are fragrant; your name is oil poured out; therefore virgins love you" (1:3).

Not only was Solomon handsome, but he was also known to have great character. He was upright and wise; the word on the street was that he was a good man, a *godly* man. The other women didn't think he was a dog. He wasn't known as lazy or incompetent. He hadn't played around with the hearts and minds of other women. His name was like oil poured out—like an offering, in other words. When people heard Solomon's name, it "went down smooth." It was pleasing, fragrant.

Now we are going deeper than the surface. What good is it in the eyes of the Lord, whose estimation matters most, if we look great but our reputations are lousy? Only one of those things will last.

Therefore, our physical attraction should always be held in check by the character of the person to whom we are attracted. In Proverbs, we find valuable instructions given to King Lemuel by his mother. As king, Lemuel could have had his pick of the fairest beauties in the land. But his mother's reminder was wise: "An excellent wife who can find? She is far more precious than jewels" (31:10).

This translation actually does not do justice fully to the verse. The NET Bible reads, "Who can find a wife of noble character? For her value is far more than rubies." In the translation of "noble character, it is the same word used in Ruth to describe her as a 'woman of valor.'"[5]

Now we are seeing how much more complex attraction ought to be when guided by the Word of God. Physical attraction is good but only outwardly important; character, on the other hand, is a matter of internal importance and should be valued as greater than jewels.

We see something similar in 1 Peter 3:3–4. Here, Peter encouraged wives in the way of prioritizing inner beauty over outer beauty, and wrote:

> Do not let your adorning be external—the braiding of hair and the putting on of gold jewelry, or the clothing you wear—but let your adorning be the hidden person of the heart with the imperishable beauty of a gentle and quiet spirit, which in God's sight is very precious.

As this passage was written directly to wives, it can be somewhat ambiguous for dating and initial romantic attraction, and bear in mind that when this was written, most marriages were arranged, and physical attraction was not of the highest concern. However, by examining this passage fully, we can clearly see that the idea of beauty for the wife should be focused more on the internal. External beauty is fine, but we must move past it and see what's in the soul of a person, who he or she actually is, and what that individual is made of.

Several years ago I saw a television show called *Caught on Camera*. It featured clips of people being secretly filmed doing all manner of horrific things, precisely because they thought they were alone. In one scene a man urinated into a pot of coffee that had been brewed for his coworkers. In another, a cook in a restaurant spit into a meal he was preparing for customers. And in yet another scene, a woman threw a puppy across a room. The show was disgusting, but it revealed that a lot goes on in a person's heart and head that simply can't be seen. In our brave, new surveillance culture, we catch the real character of people all the time, as "nanny cams" capture abuse of children and the elderly, and security cameras film employee vandalism and cruelty.

It is certainly true that the measure of a man's character is what he would do if he knew he never would be found out. Or character is, as Bill Hybels said, "who you are when no one's looking."[6] Everyone has a public face and a private face. As a friendship begins between you and some handsome man or beautiful woman, you need to see if there is real depth of character. When the beauty fades, what integrity will remain?

We can always adjust our outer appearance. Our culture has advanced in the ways of makeup and hairstyles and beauty products, but we've also added cosmetic surgery, health-food culture, and fitness programs bordering on cults. We don't all look great, but we can all look a little "better" with a little work. But the inner us? That will come out. We can't hide it forever. In times of intimacy, in times of stress, in times of struggle, there's no putting makeup on a terrible personality. There's no cosmetic surgery for poverty of character.

You can't hide that inner you. It's the real you.

Physical attraction, then, is not a substitute for knowing somebody, for being in relationship with him or her. And this is why relationships built on physical attraction never last and tend to be superficial, self-absorbed, and legalistic.

Abraham Lincoln once said, "Character was like a tree, and reputation like its shadow. The shadow is what we think of it; the tree was the real thing."[7] The first way we can look to see if the person we're attracted to has solid character is by evaluating his or her reputation. What do people say about her? Is he known for his godliness? (Remember that church attendance doesn't always equal godliness. There are a lot of "neat" Christian boys and girls but far fewer godly men and women.) Proverbs 22:1 says, "A good name is to be chosen rather than great riches." Reputation is the shadow of a person's character. If a person's reputation is poor, more than likely so is his or her character.

Let reputation be one of the green or red lights that leads you toward or away from a person you are considering dating.

Solomon's reputation, the shadow cast by his character, was so celebrated that the people watching his romance blossoming in the Song of Songs celebrated it. They were pleased by it: "We will exult and rejoice in you; we will extol your love more than wine; rightly do they love you" (1:4).

What do you look for in a person's reputation? Is it enough to see that people are impressed? What if he or she is merely a flatterer, or simply rich or powerful? What are some marks not just of impressive character but godly character?

For these, we have to look counter to the way of our culture once again. What the Bible lays out as the marks of godly character are so often diametrically opposed to the expectations and celebrations of the world. And one of the first aspects the Song of Solomon presents as commendable for a romantic relationship is one of the most despised by our broken culture.

SUBMISSION TO AUTHORITY

Is there any arguing that in our world there is an abominably low view of authority and submission? Modern society, which actually relies on the dynamic of authority and submission to survive, seems so often emotionally allergic to it! The air we breathe is this: "No one tells me what to do. I do what I want to do. No one is the boss of me."

Every generation's pop music has become increasingly anti-authoritarian. (You could, of course, say that rock-and-roll music itself subsists on a spirit of rebellion.) One example comes from the most influential rock band of all time, the Beatles, who characterized the need to change the world with their song "Revolution." The Beatles' leading cultural revolutionary, John Lennon, gave the world a song called "Imagine." It's a very pretty song, but the whole thing is about how the world might benefit if there was no religion, no government, no borders, no hell, no heaven, nothing but "peace." There has probably never been another song so simultaneously high-minded and low intellect. But it struck a resonant chord for those coming out of the countercultural sixties and seventies.

The eighties gave us "Authority Song" by John Mellencamp. "I fight authority," Mellencamp sings, "and authority always wins." He goes on to say, "Well I've been doing it since I was a young kid, and I always come out grinning."

The philosophy of antiauthority is so pervasive that it has driven major movements in arts and entertainment, politics and culture. The most recent cultural example is probably what the media have dubbed the "Occupy Movement," which is predicated on the idea that the few people who are said to own 99 percent of the wealth in the West need to be divested of all their "ill-gotten" gains. But the sentiment runs so much deeper than wealth inequality or social status. Each of us, deep down in our hearts, has an antiauthoritarian streak a mile wide. And the idea of submission makes us nervous, fearful, stubborn, and even angry.

Of course, this resistance to the idea of authority and submission is totally informed by the reality that many people throughout the ages have abused their positions of authority. When a sinner is in charge, his leadership is influenced by his sin. There are no exceptions to this. And while many virtuous leaders by God's grace have employed their authority in honorable ways, none of them have done so perfectly. For the rest, however, the abuses of authority, toxic leadership, dictatorial excesses, and exploitation of power have complicated and soured the general culture of authority and submission that the Bible establishes as an inherently good system. It's good for government, good for the church, good for the home. But when those in authority abuse their authority, those in submission suffer. And it makes submission more and more a scary prospect.

We should say without hesitation that when a person exalts himself or herself beyond all authority and tradition, he or she is walking outside of God's design. Authority is not bad; *abuse* of authority is bad. God gave us institutions and authorities to help shape us and protect us. So we have to ask, as we consider a member of the opposite sex for romantic relationship, what is his reputation as it pertains to authority and submission? Is she in glad submission to any authorities over her? Has he placed himself under the authority of a local church? Is she in covenant with other church members? Does he submit to his pastors? How does she treat older men and women?

Look to see if your prospective significant other is his own authority. See if she bristles or blossoms under proper authority. If you can't tell, or if it doesn't seem as though he has any authority at all, I would pump the brake on the relationship.

A woman who is functionally her own god won't have the ability to hear from others about blind spots and errors in her life. A man who cannot gladly submit to his leaders likely cannot be expected to exercise a humble authority in his home. A woman who rebels against leadership cannot be expected to practice honorable submission in her home.

Continuing in Song of Solomon chapter 1, we see something peculiar in verses 5–6:

> I am very dark, but lovely,
>> O daughters of Jerusalem,
> like the tents of Kedar,
>> like the curtains of Solomon.
> Do not gaze at me because I am dark,
>> because the sun has looked upon me.
> My mother's sons were angry with me;
>> they made me keeper of the vineyards,
>> but my own vineyard I have not kept!

There is some complexity to these two verses, but essentially, the woman was expressing some insecurity about the darkness of her skin. She had not, in her estimation, had much opportunity to care for her complexion—to keep up her "beauty regimen," in other words—because she spent a lot of time outdoors. And what was she doing? Tending to the family business, apparently. Some Bible scholars debate whether the "mother's sons" who are angry with her are the woman's actual brothers or her cultural kinsmen—other potential suitors, actually—who did not desire her because of her sun-darkened complexion. In other words, she may have been saying, "None of the other boys have been attracted to me because I have spent more time working in the fields than in tending to my beauty."

In any event, we see two primary things about her character here: she was a hard worker, submitting herself to the needs of her family above the desires of vanity, and she had a humble insecurity about her appearance. She was not vain.

COMMITMENT

One of the things I noticed when I was in college ministry was the large group of students who wouldn't commit to anything—a college major, a gym, a church, a place to live, a group of friends. The only thing they seemed committed to was being noncommittal. Every semester the talk would turn to another school they might transfer to, a new major they were going to try out, or a new part-time job they were interested in (because, you know, their current one was lame). This group was always holding out for something better and didn't want to miss out on anything that *might* be happening somewhere else. They were unstable. And this instability cost them the joy of *knowing* and *being known*.

In Song of Solomon 1:7, we read this: "Tell me, you whom my soul loves, where you pasture your flock, where you make it lie down at noon."

The woman is equating "love from the soul" with a commitment to her partner's presence. Wherever he is pasturing his flock, wherever he is providing a place of rest and nourishment and provision, that's where she wants to be. There is an indication here of the desire to commit.

Obviously, when you are first attracted to someone, you don't make inappropriate commitments, but you do want to see before you pursue someone in a potentially romantic way if he or she is inclined toward commitment. The woman in this Song wants to commit to her suitor's pasture; for her, the grass is not always greener on the other side of the fence.

As you consider the person you are physically attracted to, look for evidence of commitment in his or her life. Has he joined and become committed to a local church? Does she have a deepening relationship with a group of friends? How is his relationship with his family?

I think that church membership is a huge consideration, precisely because there is no such thing as a perfect church, and in our day and age in the West, we have so many options to choose from. Churches are full of sinners, so there will always be some messiness in a church. Churches are like families that way. So when a person stays in a church for a long period of time, there is evidence that she has been able to see that everything's not perfect, but she nevertheless said, "I'm going to stay. I'm going to try to make this work. My commitment is more important than my desire to run away."

If you find someone who is rootless, always looking for what's next, always looking for "better than"—better job, better group of friends, better church, better hobby, better *whatever*—you should be extremely cautious.

What you're looking for is a deep rootedness, or at least a deep capacity for rootedness. Obviously among young adults there is much that is in transition in relation to school and jobs and so on. But despite the transient nature of that particular stage of life, are there signs of deep commitment? If there is no evidence of commitment in his or her life, I would caution you to move very slowly into any kind of serious relationship.

Because the Bible tells us we need to go deeper than physical attraction in our relationships, and because we know that what we find physically attractive has been for the most part culturally informed, it is wise to acknowledge that God has hardwired us for the commitment of *companionship* over and above sexual attraction or physical pleasure. Companionship brings deeper joy and greater pleasure than the mere physical could ever bring by itself.

If you have physical attraction and no companionship in your relationship, you'll eventually be miserable; but if you have deep companionship with each other, physical attraction isn't as important and becomes less and less so as time passes.

In the movie *Cast Away*, we see a stark depiction of a person's innate hunger for companionship. The main character, Chuck

Noland, is involved in a plane crash. He survives but ends up stranded on a deserted island. As his loneliness wears on him, Chuck finds a volleyball that floated ashore, draws a face on it, and has conversations with it over the course of his time on the island.

After a number of years of isolation and a failed suicide attempt, Chuck builds a raft to try to get off the island. Following his successful launch, he encounters and overcomes a great storm. The next day, once the waters had calmed, his constant companion, Wilson, the volleyball, falls off the raft. In perhaps the most powerful scene of the movie, Chuck begins to weep uncontrollably because of the anguish of losing his only "friend." Through this brief scene, director Robert Zemeckis laid bare the undeniable ache in every human heart for companionship. It is a beautifully powerful portrayal of a need, which supersedes the mere desire for sexual gratification or "attraction." It truly is "not good that the man should be alone" (Gen. 2:18).

In the end, of course, it is Jesus who provides this perfect companionship for his children. "No longer do I call you servants," he said in John 15:15, "but I have called you friends." Through him we see that the commitment we make to our brothers and sisters in the church far outweighs even the good gifts of marriage and sexual fulfillment. Marriage and sex will pass away (see Matt. 22:30), but our commitment as friends—as family!—with the saints of God will endure forever.

Can your prospective partner commit? His or her physical attractiveness is a good thing, but it's not an enduring thing—the ability to commit may carry the weight of eternity.

SUFFERING

Embedded in a person's ability to commit is his or her ability to endure in suffering. You can look for evidence of someone's "commitment ability" by observing how he or she handles times of stress, hardship, or brokenness.

Helen Keller once said, "Character cannot be developed in ease and quiet. Only through experience of trial and suffering can the soul be strengthened, ambition inspired and success achieved." The apostle James put it this way:

> Count it all joy, my brothers, when you meet trials
> of various kinds, for you know that the testing of
> your faith produces steadfastness. And let steadfast-
> ness have its full effect, that you may be perfect and
> complete, lacking in nothing. (1:2–4)

Most people are pleasant when the world is going the way they want. But a person's character can be seen most clearly when the brokenness of the world has invaded his or her peace, when the way he or she thinks things ought to be is interrupted, disrupted, and dismantled.

How does your partner respond to betrayal, to drama in her family, to arguments between friends? How does he behave when he is stressed, sick, frustrated, or tired? You're not looking for perfection, of course, because everyone except Jesus has responded to difficulty in ways that are out of step with the gospel. We are all sinners, and over time we engage in responses that are less than godly. But in times of challenge, does the person you're attracted to circle back around and own her sin? Does she repent for her ungodly responses and seek forgiveness? How prone to anger is he? There is a reason why when a church is looking for leaders, it specifically excludes the quick-tempered (see Titus 1:7).

In times of stress, the fractures in our projected images appear. The real us—the one inside—is revealed. Speaking about suffering, the apostle Paul wrote in 2 Corinthians 4, "But we have this treasure in jars of clay, to show that the surpassing power belongs to God and not to us." The image here is one of a fragile container broken open in hardship. When we are broken open in suffering, what we truly treasure (what we worship) is revealed. Paul continued:

> We are afflicted in every way, but not crushed;
> perplexed, but not driven to despair; persecuted,
> but not forsaken; struck down, but not destroyed;
> always carrying in the body the death of Jesus, so
> that the life of Jesus may also be manifested in our
> bodies. (vv. 8–10)

When the person you're attracted to goes through something difficult, it is evidence of her humanity if she is sad, stressed, or wounded. But what she does with that sadness, stress, and woundedness makes all the difference between someone who treasures Christ as supreme and satisfying and one who is her own god, who lives with a sense of entitlement and worships comfort.

If you are seeking a romantic relationship, be wise and keep things with a prospective partner in the "friend zone" until you have seen how he handles the stress of a broken and fallen world. Because there is no avoiding the stress and fallenness of the world, *especially in the covenant commitment of marriage!* When we commit to a spouse for life, we are agreeing to enter a sacred union between two sinners and Jesus, and when you've got two sinners walking together over the years, you will see just how sinful he or she—and you—can be. Tim Keller said, "Marriage is the Mack truck driving through your life, revealing your flaws and humbling your reactions."[8] Yes, and in fact, marriage can itself sometimes *be* the "suffering" that breaks us open to reveal what we truly worship.

After surveying the character of a potential partner, if you find out that his reputation is not great, she isn't very godly, he seems commitment-phobic, or she does not handle stress well, yet you're still attracted to this person, you should ask yourself why. What is it that you are worshipping that would draw you toward romantic intimacy and potential commitment with someone of unhealthy character? Is it possible you are thinking superficially? Are your values tied to things that don't last?

If you can say yes to any of those questions, there is great hope for you.

One of my fears in writing this book is that by pointing out the wisdom in the Song of Songs, many of us who are guilty of foolishness might feel condemned and lose heart. But I want to end each chapter of our journey through the Song by looking at how the gospel's call to confession and repentance enters our mess and removes the weight of guilt and shame by pointing us to Jesus. We read about one of the biggest relational disasters in the Bible in 2 Samuel 11, where King David saw Bathsheba bathing, was compelled by her beauty, and with no thought of the repercussions of his actions, sent for her. He coveted another man's wife, abused his authority by having her brought to him, and committed adultery with her.

If that wasn't bad enough, he then arranged to have her husband, Uriah, moved to the front lines of battle to increase his chance of death. Uriah was killed, and David, by intention, became a murderer. In the aftermath of sin upon sin, David took Bathsheba as his wife.

In 2 Samuel 12, Nathan confronted David, and David erupted in tears under the weight of his conviction. He repented of his sin against the Lord. Although there were plenty of circumstantial consequences for David's rebellion against God (see 2 Sam. 12:10–12, 14), David was forgiven by God and was still called a man after God's own heart (see Acts 13:22). What a thing to say about a man guilty of lust, adultery, deception, and murder—and those are only the most obvious of his sins! That this kind of person could in the end be declared a man after God's own heart is a testimony not to the greatness of David but to the greatness of God.

There is no sin—past, present, or future—that has more power than the cross of Jesus Christ. Whatever darkness from your past or trouble or guilt from your present bothers you as you progress through this book, please know that you haven't strayed too far that there is no redemption for you. Full reconciliation and healing are abundantly available for you in Christ Jesus. The man who knew no sin took our sin to the cross so that we might be clothed in his perfect righteousness and completely justified before God the Father. God has seen our unloveliness—the deep brokenness and rebellion in our hearts—and instead of withdrawing, he pursues us to the beautiful end. He made an eternal commitment to sinners because of his great love for us. And because grace is true, you can face the world with all of its dangers and troubles, knowing you have been established forever as blameless by the holy groom, Jesus Christ.

CHAPTER TWO

DATING

What we have seen so far in the Song of Solomon is that dance of consideration and imagination we call attraction. A woman looked at King Solomon and found him desirable. The attraction was mutual. Next, the two of them began to consider each other's character and imagine what a romantic relationship might be like. Part of this consideration involved spending time together to "test the waters," to see if the attraction was only skin-deep, to see if the initial appraisal of the other's character was accurate.

We've all been attracted to someone before. We know what it is like to have that initial captivation, to find somebody pleasing to see and to be around. When we want to become intentional about pursuing this attraction further, we begin to find ways to hang out with each other. We watch how the other person lives his or her life. Most of us, if we are thinking wisely, will not be too quick to throw our hearts out there. We exercise patience and consideration.

At this point in chapter 1 of the Song of Songs, we have not seen a serious entry into what we might call "dating," or what historically would be called "courtship," but more of a testing the waters to see if they should jump in.

If a person's reputation is good and you have seen in the person a willingness to submit to others, to commit to things, to see things through, and if you've watched her navigate difficult days with character and wisdom, then it's not a bad thing to seek her out and consider moving deeper into the relationship. And this is exactly what happens in chapter 1, verse 7:

> Tell me, you whom my soul loves,
> > where you pasture your flock,
> > where you make it lie down at noon;
> for why should I be like one who veils herself
> > beside the flocks of your companions?

This was no longer just physical attraction but a mixture of physical attraction and delight in the character of a person. She asked the question, "Where are you going to be?" The reason she asked is because she planned on being there too!

If you are single, you know that can be a risky question. We have already seen her anxiety over the way she looks, but she now boldly asks. She wants to hang out in a more meaningful way. And of course, it's quite natural for a relationship to grow in this way. We can call this the dating stage.

Dating in our day and age—let's just be honest—is *goofy*. It can sort of be like selling a used car. We try to hide anything that may make a sale less likely and advertise only what will "close the deal." And what closes the deal in the modern dating world is almost always sex. Thus, dating becomes a lot about hiding who you really are, hiding your imperfections, and in many cases, unfortunately, displaying and making primary what ought to be reserved only for marriage. Things have certainly changed over the decades, and while human beings aren't any more lustful today than they've always been, our cultural standards and romantic ideals have certainly degraded to the point where the lustful desires have become more prominent, even more *driving*.

Historically speaking, a dating relationship began with an expectation and hope that a person would either stumble across or be introduced to someone of the opposite sex who had the potential for compatibility. The two would begin spending time together, gradually getting to know each other first in social settings, and then spending more one-on-one time together in conversation and recreation. That was dating in decades past. But traditional dating is becoming more and more rare, and a culture of hooking up has emerged in its place.

While technology has begun to play a large role in how people meet (and certainly has both pros and cons), the dark side of today's approach to dating is not really dating at all. For all of our romantic aspirations and relationship advice in magazines, books, movies, and blogs, our culture suffers the unfortunate rise of "hooking up." What exactly does that mean? Hooking up is defined as "a sexual encounter which may or may not include sexual intercourse, usually occurring between people who are strangers or brief acquaintances."[1] It is when men and women seek shallow relationships for the sole purpose of sex.

The stats on this hookup culture are staggering. One study reveals that 77.7 percent of college females admitted to "hooking up."[2] This means that these young women connect with young men they either don't know at all or barely know for the sole purpose of physical gratification. For males, the percentage is even higher—84.2 percent.[3]

If sex is what God says it is, then there are few things as damaging to the human soul as casual sexual encounters. The hookup culture is yet another symptom of a confused and broken society that has elevated the role of physical gratification and sex beyond the biblical norms and wasted them, sacrificing contentment and joy on the altar of momentary pleasure—leaving only brokenness and regret.

It should be apparent to clear-thinking Christians that today's young people must navigate the dating world with more caution than the generations before us. Believers pursuing romantic relationships perhaps now more than ever need to remember Jesus's words in Matthew 10:16: "Behold, I am sending you out as sheep in the midst of wolves, so be wise as serpents and innocent as doves."

To help you develop this wisdom and innocence, I want to cover some important considerations when it comes to dating. If you are pursuing a romantic relationship into the dating stage, here are some things that should always be present.

RECIPROCITY

In Song of Solomon 1:7, the woman asked Solomon where he was going to be so she could be there too. Look at his response in verse 8: "If you do not know, O most beautiful among women, follow in the tracks of the flock, and pasture your young goats beside the shepherds' tents." Notice that Solomon didn't respond by telling her he would text her later, only to forget, or inform her he was busy with the guys. Instead, he was playful and (appropriately) flirtatious, encouraging her to find him.

This should go without saying, but in our world, it probably warrants being said: in dating there must be *reciprocity*. If you want to move from the "friend zone" into dating, the object of your desire has to want the same thing. It is never okay to stalk or hound a person who doesn't feel the same way you do about the nature of your relationship. I have often watched young men and women make each other very uncomfortable when they continue to pursue and attempt to woo someone long after a clear "I'm not interested" has been given.

Men, the Bible commands us in 1 Timothy 5:2 to treat older women as mothers and younger women as sisters. I don't know if you have sisters, but I have two. My younger sister didn't have a date until I graduated and left home, and at that point, dudes came out of the woodwork! It was as though they were just waiting for me to bail. But when I *was* around, I had several friends who were interested in dating my sister. One guy named Brent flat out asked me, "Hey, man, would you mind if I dated your sister?" It was pretty big of him to even ask, but of course I responded, "Yes, I very, very much mind. I would like you to not be anywhere near my sister."

Maybe I was overprotective, but I think, in general, this is how we ought to consider every woman—as a sister to look out for. We should want to protect, encourage, and love. It's never okay to make a woman feel unsafe. It's never okay to pressure a woman, to make a situation so uncomfortable that she has to avoid you. If she says,

"This ain't happening," then it's not happening. Our default posture toward women should always be to honor them.

Women, in the same way, if you are trying to pursue a romantic path with a man and he's indicating that's not the path he wants to take with you, throwing down ultimatums or trying to seduce him is foolishness. It is foolishness that *might* win you some affection in the short term, but in the end, it will produce regret and resentment and disaster. Don't do it.

There must be reciprocity to move out of the friend zone. If a person is clear that he or she is not interested in you romantically, learn to trust that God has someone better for you than you have imagined for yourself.

Most of us are pretty clear that forcing ourselves on someone, even if just emotionally, is wrong. But too often we become so wrapped up in our emotions and desire for romantic fulfillment that we go beyond where our hearts are meant to and therefore sometimes take our bodies where they ought not go. Sometimes the object of our attraction is more than willing to reciprocate in the way of physical intimacy but not in the way of Christlikeness and godly romance. This is not the kind of reciprocity you should look for. As you pursue a relationship into the world of dating, don't simply look for someone who reciprocates your attraction but one who reciprocates your desire to honor Jesus in your relationship above all else.

LIFE-GIVING IMPACT

In 1:9–10, Solomon's response left no ambiguity about his intentions. "I compare you, my love, to a mare among Pharaoh's chariots.

Your cheeks are lovely with ornaments, your neck with strings of jewels."

It seems like an odd compliment to compare a woman to a horse, doesn't it? There are several lines throughout the Song that I would not advise using on your significant other, and calling your girl a horse is probably one of those. But, in context, Solomon was very much complimenting her. He spoke to her insecurities, establishing clarity about his desire to be with her in the same way she wanted to be with him.

Not only is there reciprocity in this book—they shared an attraction—but they also were intent on nurturing each other emotionally and spiritually. This is the first sign that their relationship was going to be life-giving. Here's how I know this to be true: Pharaoh's horses were always white Arabian horses.

My oldest daughter rides horses. She has a brown quarter horse named Gypsy, and at the stable where she keeps her, there's also a white Arabian, Toi. Toi is spectacular. When we drive out to the barn or past the pasture, I can't always see Gypsy because there are ten or eleven other horses out there, and Gypsy the brown quarter horse just kind of blends in with the background. But you can always see Toi.

Toi stands in stark contrast to the rest of his surroundings. He doesn't blend in. White, powerful, beautiful, easy to spot. And this is what Solomon was saying to this woman: "I see you. When I look around, you stand out to me. You don't blend into the crowd. You're the one that my eyes go to. You are unique. You are eye-catching. I am drawn to you. You are not like the rest."

Do you see how this might be like water to an insecure soul? Theirs was a life-giving relationship. He didn't capitalize on her insecurities but instead brought the good news of his approval to her.

The deepest cries of our hearts so often can be characterized by a desperate desire for our whole selves to be known *and at the same time* delighted in. Solomon said to his prospective partner, "I see the things you're insecure about, and I find you absolutely captivating. You impress me and please me." That was life-giving.

Those of you who are pursuing a dating relationship right now, if your attraction has given way to a relationship that's making you miserable, a relationship that's emotionally exhausting and spiritually compromised, a relationship that's a culmination of mixed signals and tears and confusion, I think you ought to get out. If the relationship is wearying, life sucking, or lacks clarity and intention, or if someone is just playing games with you, I would hit the brakes hard. The harsh reality is that behavior in these kinds of relationships doesn't get better over time; *it gets worse.* Familiarity will not breed better behavior. The further you go together, the less guarded you will become. At the beginning of a dating relationship, people tend to be on their best behavior to give the best impression. If at the beginning your romantic interest's "best" is pretty bad, you can bet it will get only worse.

APPROVAL BY GODLY COUNSEL

What we see next in our look at the Song of Songs is the excitement and joy that *others* had about their dating relationship: "We will make for you ornaments of gold, studded with silver" (1:11). The friends of the couple in this text weren't fearful for the hearts and souls of these two as they grew closer; they were excited.

One sure way to walk in foolishness in a romantic relationship is to date someone who troubles the godly counselors in your life.

There was once a beautiful young woman at The Village who began a friendship with a young man who attended the church off and on but seemed to have no real love for the Lord or fruit in his life. He was charming, had a great sense of humor, and was doing well at the firm that employed him. Friends of this young woman noticed how she was drawn to him and gently reminded her that her desire should be for a godly man who would love, serve, and lead her toward a greater intimacy with Christ, not someone who was, for all intents and purposes, lukewarm about his faith. But the young woman ignored her friends' advice and began dating the guy.

Once again, her friends appealed to her to reconsider pursuing the relationship, and once again, she refused to listen. Instead, she found a different group of friends who wouldn't disagree with her choices, claiming all along that she could influence him for good.

Not long after they began dating, they started crossing lines she had never intended to cross, and the relationship turned almost entirely physical. And toxic. After about eight months, she discovered he was cheating on her, and her heart was shattered. She felt foolish and ashamed. In her brokenness, she nervously limped back to the friends who had warned her, pleaded with her, and prayed for her, fearing an "I told you so" or an "If you would have only listened …," but instead she found grace, empathy, and compassion. This sweet sister is still struggling, still wounded, but she found a safe harbor in which to heal with the friends God has given her.

Proverbs 12:15 says, "The way of a fool is right in his own eyes, but a wise man listens to advice." The men or women with whom you are doing life, the ones you have shared your struggles, hopes, and dreams with, the ones who have prayed for you, encouraged you, and spoken into your life—what do they think about your relationship? Are they rejoicing or cringing? Obviously it's your life, but God has given you these men and women as a gift for your support and protection. Our godly friends, family members, and especially our pastors, elders, and other spiritual leaders very often see things about our relationships that we can't, or sometimes *refuse,* to see. As people who love us and who are accountable to God for caring for our walk with Christ, they should be honest about problematic relationships. So ask these people in your life for their perspective and counsel.

If they are not supportive of the relationship, fight the urge to find people who are more "supportive"—people who really just tell you what you want to hear—and instead heed the advice of godly counsel and let your relationship with the prospective partner be one simply of friendship, nothing more.

THOUGHTS OF YOU

Song of Solomon 1:12–14 is a bit tricky. The passage sounds erotic and sensual, and there is no doubt some of that kind of desire was building (as we will see shortly), but what's happened immediately in this text wasn't explicit. Our woman said this: "While the king was on his couch, my nard gave forth its fragrance. My beloved is to me a sachet of myrrh that lies between my breasts. My beloved is to me a cluster of henna blossoms in the vineyards of Engedi."

She was lying in bed and thinking of Solomon. She wasn't having sexual fantasies about him, but she was "crushing" on him, so to speak. In Solomon's day, women who could afford it wore a little leather pouch, called a nard, around their necks, often filled with fragrant objects, like a substitute for perfume. In verses 12–14, our woman was speaking symbolically, saying that Solomon was the fragrant object around her neck. She was not saying he was actually there in the bed with her, lying between her breasts. She was saying that he brought "fragrance" to her life, to her spirit. When she thought about him, she was in her "happy place," smelling flowers and strolling through the blossoming vineyards.

Solomon had just told her he thought she was a knockout (see 1:8–10), and she was swooning. They carried each other in their romantic daydreams. It was difficult for them to be apart without thinking of one another.

One important application from this line of thinking is remembering that where there is no mutual initiative, where there is no thoughtful concern and care for each other, the relationship is already dying. I have a story from my own life that, much to my shame, proves that point.

When I was in college, I was close friends with a young woman I liked very much. But that's all we were—friends. I loved hanging out with her. She was godly, she was beautiful, but I just wasn't attracted to her in a romantic way. The problem was that she didn't want to stay in the friend zone. So one day, she gave me an ultimatum. She said, "Look, I like you. It's apparent I like you in a way that you don't like me. So we can't be 'just friends' anymore." In my foolishness and cowardice, I suggested that we date because I didn't want to lose her companionship. But I knew she was way more interested in me than I was in her. This truth really became apparent when I went out of town for about three days, and I hardly thought of her. I finally called her, but only because I knew I was supposed to.

This particular woman was not interested in playing games or hanging out in the "sort of dating, sort of not dating" category. When it came to the idea of our relationship, she was not thinking, *I could take it or leave it.* In fact, she sent me a letter at my hotel, and when I got home, I found a little package of my favorite candy waiting.

I felt sick to my stomach. And I remember thinking, *I am a horrible person.*

We were in an unfair situation where, as the man, I was not showing any initiative in the relationship, just being halfhearted and too lazy to be honest. She was showing *all* the initiative. And I knew that would hurt her heart in the long run. In the end, I finally manned up, sat down with her, asked for forgiveness, and ended the relationship. It was awful. I wounded her in some deep ways.

She deserved a man who thought about her as much as she thought about him, whose actions toward her were not careless and self-centered but purposeful and affectionate. As a father of daughters and as the husband of my wife, I think back on that situation with regret.

So I'll say this to you: if you're in a dating relationship and the other person is showing little to no initiative, the relationship is already broken and you're on the clock. If you're driving everything and the other person is driving nothing, you're headed over the relational cliff.

Be honest with yourself. Do you think often about the other person? Are you considerate? Do you miss him or her when you're away from each other? If there is an indifference on either side of the relationship—if it seems like one of you could "take or leave" the other—downshift back into the friend zone.

SAFETY AND PURITY

In Song of Solomon 1:16–17, Solomon said this: "Behold, you are beautiful, my beloved, truly delightful. Our couch is green; the beams of our house are cedar; our rafters are pine."

On the surface, this may not sound like it has much meaning, but the scene our man set is a very important one, and it gives us further insight into the care given to their relationship, as romantic and affectionate as it was.

Let me set up the explanation of this text this way: Nearly every Christian dating couple knows the inherent foolishness of "movie night." This happens over and over again, more times than any of us can count. I've had this conversation so often that I can rehearse it easily. A young man and woman are dating, and one asks, "What do you want to do tonight?" The other replies, "I don't know; let's go grab something to eat." So they grab something to eat. Then one says, "Well, why don't we just go to your place and watch a movie?"

Now, can we all just be honest here? Nothing good and godly ever happens between dating couples when they lie on a couch together late at night to watch a movie. It has never in the history of humankind led to discussions about cinematography or the symbolic resonance of the director's body of work or whatever. It starts with snuggling, and then it turns into mouth to mouth, hands to body, and then progresses until one of you gets a cooler head, or you both lose your heads altogether.

But Solomon and his bride knew enough not to trust one another's impulses. They were very attracted to each other, and they *knew* this. What was actually happening in 1:16–17 was indicative of the safety and purity in the couple's physical relationship.

A deeper look at where they were hanging out shows us they were outside: "Our couch is green," he said (1:16). They were in the park. They were in public. "The beams of our house are cedar; our rafters are pine" (1:17). And Solomon was the one initiating this public setting.

So often in dating relationships, it is the man who pushes, tempts, and leads the way into lust—not always, but very often. But here in the Song, Solomon took the initiative toward purity and safety.

As you date, there will naturally be a growing desire for physical intimacy with your partner. Please understand: *this is not a bad thing!* It doesn't make you gross or evil or perverted or wrong. You have a desire for physical intimacy because God instilled it within you. Desire is not in itself bad, but it must be held in check until marriage.

Remember, God is the creator of sex; he invented it. And it is not God's desire to keep from you any pleasure but rather to lead you into the fullest pleasure possible. So with that said, be careful not to put yourself in harm's way.

Ten o'clock. The two of you alone in an apartment, cuddled on a couch, watching some movie—this is not going to lead to righteousness. It's just not safe. The dating relationship should be safe, and there should be a pursuit in it for purity, led intentionally by the man. Therefore, men, don't put the burden on your girlfriend or fiancée to keep turning down your advances or reminding you of God's design for sex. Don't put her in that position. You lead, and do so in a way that protects you both from sexual temptation.

PROMISE OF A FUTURE

Next, we enter the second chapter of the Song of Solomon, which continues with the woman's declaration: "I am a rose of Sharon, a lily of the valleys." And he responded, "As a lily among brambles, so is my love among the young women" (vv. 1–2).

Here is a woman who had a growing sense of her own identity because of the progression of the relationship. She wasn't left confused, doubting, wondering, or lost. Solomon did not give her mixed signals or a broken heart. She didn't compromise her beliefs or question her faith. She did not worry about his intentions or try to decipher his advances.

In so many dating relationships today, we see how the mishandling of a woman's heart ends up withering and wearying her, how emotional (and physical) mistreatment makes a woman feel less herself. But this doesn't happen with Solomon's betrothed. The way he led their relationship and the way he poured into her heart left her confident and self-assured. She blossomed.

They were out in public, going on dates. He said, "You're beautiful; you're delightful." He created clarity in their relationship about his feelings, his intentions, and his pursuit. She could only respond then by basically saying, "There's no question that I am above the other ladies, that I am yours, that you are mine, and that there's something sweet going on here."

It is a dangerous thing to surrender the deepest parts of your heart to someone who has not provided this kind of clarity for you. If your dating relationship is going to move forward, if things are going to get more serious, there *must* be clarity.

Look at verse 3: "As an apple tree among the trees of the forest, so is my beloved among the young men. With great delight I sat in his shadow, and his fruit was sweet to my taste." Not only was their relationship safe and pure, not only was there clarity, but she had a growing sense of ease and safety around him. She was comfortable in his presence, not nervous or frightened. The way he handled her, the way he walked with her, the way they talked, the way they spent time together all gave her the evidence she needed to know that inside of him lay a desire to protect her physically, emotionally, and spiritually.

"He brought me to the banqueting house, and his banner over me was love" (v. 4). What a thing to say! She exulted in the way he wooed her. The "banqueting house" speaks to the way she felt nurtured by him, *fed* by him as it were. He gave her the royal treatment. And over their relationship waved not the banner of lust but of love—selfless, sacrificial, spiritual love.

"His banner over me was love." This also indicates that Solomon was not in denial about their relationship. He wasn't trying to keep her on the down-low. He proudly declared his love for this woman. He didn't say, "Hey, this is my buddy, the Shulammite woman." He said, "Hey, everybody, this is my girl!" He changed his Facebook status, and he let the world know he was off the market.

Thus, their relationship was moving forward.

If you are in a relationship where the other person refuses to acknowledge openly that his pursuit of you, delight in you, and enjoyment of you goes beyond how he feels about the nine other women you see him with, then you are not really dating. You are being played. You are caught in a game in which your heart is going to lose.

But for those relationships where the appropriate boundaries are in place, where dating is giving way to something more intentional and serious, the heart becomes fuller and more overflowing with love and affection.

We see in the progression of the Song more and more affirmation that sexual desire is good for couples pursuing marriage because it bodes well for their sexual health once the marriage covenant has sanctified their sexual expression with each other.

I love that the Bible never pulls any punches but is always honest with us. "Sustain me with raisins," the Shulammite woman said. "Refresh me with apples, for I am sick with love. His left hand is under my head, and his right hand embraces me!" (vv. 5–6). Because of all of his kindness, his clarity, and his godly pursuit, she has an acknowledged and growing desire for his sexual touch.

In this time in Israel's history, raisins and apples were considered sensual foods; they were even thought to help women get pregnant.

David was said to have given apples and raisins to his men who were returning home from war as a great reward for them and their wives. It was a way of saying, "Go home, brothers, and make babies!"

The Shulammite woman was basically saying, "I'm in. I need some raisins! A girl needs some apples right now!"

Because she trusted Solomon's intentions and they were committed to "not stir up or awaken love until it pleases" (v. 7), she was free to acknowledge her growing desire.

It's important for me to repeat this to you because of the mixed messages the church has historically sent young people about sex: it is not wrong to have a growing desire for sexual touch. I'm going to keep coming back to this truth before our study of this book is over because we are told so many times that sex is bad, wrong, sinful, gross. And then we are expected to embrace it fully when we marry. That message is not a great way to set a couple free to marital intimacy. And the couples who desire help many times have to go to the world to find it. But the world doesn't know how to correctly handle something God designed because it doesn't know God.

Sometimes I meet young men who despair of their sexual appetites and say things like, "I just want God to take this away from me!" And I always say, "You really don't."

What they should want God to do is empower their discipline and strength to be obedient, because sexual desire is a gift. We shouldn't ask God to take one of his gifts away from us. Rather, we should ask him to help us steward it well, and lead us into the covenant relationship where we can enjoy it according to his design.

Now, look at the next part of the verse—a word of caution: "I adjure you, O daughters of Jerusalem, by the gazelles or the does, of the field that you not stir up or awaken love until it pleases" (v. 7).

I think my friend Tommy Nelson was the first person I ever heard teach through this wonderful book, and in one of his most profound insights into the text, he compared the desire for sexual touch to a fire:

Keeping a fire going requires boundaries and appropriate fuel. In marriage, that fuel is growing respect, tenderness, admiration, mutual desires and dreams, mutual Christlike relationships with others (extended family, children, friends, business associations, community relationships), memories and traditions established over time, romance and ongoing expressions of affection, and so forth.[4]

What he was saying is that the fuel of sexual zeal within the confines of marriage arrives out of a growing knowledge of each other, a deepening understanding of each other, a study of how you can bring grace to all the ways your spouse is different and uniquely himself or herself. In some ways, watching your spouse be who God designed him or her to be, through the lens of the gospel, becomes *arousing* to you.

Women, watching your man be disciplined, watching him love your kids, watching him succeed and flourish in his work—aren't these things attractive? When you consider these things through the work of Christ, don't they make your husband seem manlier, more alluring to you?

Men, watching your wife serve you in tender ways, watching her tend to the home or pursue her gifts and interests, seeing her flourish as a creative or enterprising woman of God—isn't that sexy?

Service and godliness, seeing how your partner interacts with family members, business associates, and church communities, create respect for your spouse that goes beyond the physical. Sex within marriage can take on an entirely new dimension—that of giving to the other, including those times when sexual desire may not be so strong.

Sexual intimacy outside of marriage, however, does not have these liberating boundaries or healthy fuel. Outside of marriage, sex becomes about self-gratification and fulfilling personal desires.

Therefore, the Shulammite woman pleads with us to not awaken love until it's time (see Song of Sol. 8:4), because if you enter into the physical too quickly, you crush the ability to actually grow in legitimate intimacy.

Don't awaken love until it's time, because if you do, you will stop talking, stop digging around in the depths of each other's souls, stop trying to figure out how to communicate better, stop trying to figure out what makes the other person tick. Instead, you use each other physically. It may be enjoyable for a while, but I guarantee it will leave you hollow.

If the dating relationship is moving along and you see these healthy things we've looked at in the Song of Songs, it's important to apply a healthy dose of grace to your evaluations. Nobody is perfect at all of these things. When you are navigating a dating relationship, part of getting to know each other means working through misunderstandings and hurt feelings. Don't try to hold out for perfection, because only Jesus can offer you that. Instead, what you should ask yourself is: Does he show a trajectory of health and godliness? Is she willing to repent when she does wrong? Is he a faithful follower of Jesus Christ?

Where there is repentance and confession and seriousness about walking in the ways of the Lord, it is worth it to continue working at your relationship. But if you do, realize that dating moves forward. Dating for Christians has a specific trajectory.

When the trajectory for both partners is mutual Christlikeness, the next step is to chart the trajectory of your path as a couple. As you move from simply dating into a more serious version of dating, you arrive at what we might call courtship.

Courtship is when you're not just "dating to date" anymore, but you're dating to move toward marriage. The courting couple ask themselves and each other, "Are you and I going to be together for the rest of our lives?" As the relationship progresses into courtship, the answer is, "Yes, we believe so."

CHAPTER THREE

COURTSHIP: AN OLD IDEA REVIVED

When I began dating my now-wife, Lauren, I lived in Abilene, Texas, and she lived in Longview—about five and a half hours apart by car. At that time I worked at a church, was in school full-time, and traveled occasionally for speaking engagements. On a typical weekend, I would finish speaking Friday night around eleven o'clock, get in my car, and drive to Longview. I'd arrive at the house of Lauren's parents sometime in the early morning, sleep for a few hours, then wake up, spend time with Lauren through lunch, get back in my car, and drive home to Abilene so that I could be at church Sunday morning. I did this for a year.

It was not a very healthy or convenient schedule. But it never felt crazy to me—never. Looking back on it now, though, I think, *Man, that girl had some voodoo on me or something.* I was in the car fourteen to sixteen hours in a thirty-eight-hour period every week just to spend four or five hours with her.

Solomon and the woman he loved were in a very similar stage in their relationship. We see this in chapter 2, verse 8: "The voice of my beloved! Behold, he comes, leaping over the mountains, bounding over the hills."

There was excitement in her voice about the way Solomon treated her. He couldn't get enough of her. Every spare moment he had was spent making his way to her.

This was beyond infatuation, beyond puppy love and initial attraction. There was magnetism here. "This just might be it. I think this person is 'the one.'"

Before I met Lauren, I was always the guy who thought, *Is there really a woman out there who'll get to know the real me and still say, "Yeah, I'll spend the rest of my life with you"*? I had serious doubts about whether that woman really existed. And then all of a sudden, I met her. The kind of excitement that resulted was the kind that had me driving long distances for long periods of time as often as I could, and I never felt bothered at all by it. In fact, I felt eager and energized at the prospect. That's different from the kind of excitement I had being merely infatuated by a girl.

When you enter the "I think this is 'the one'" territory, you will leap over mountains and bound over hills to be with each other. Part of that excitement and eagerness is about more than "hanging out." It becomes more and more about "sorting out." When the excitement in a relationship moves beyond the fun of the here and now into the realm of being together for life, you start having deeper conversations—*marriage* conversations. Not all of these discussions are easy to have. Some can be very difficult. But when the dating stage begins to get more serious, there is no longer an avoidance of the difficult stuff. A couple will begin having conversations in categories such as these:

- The Past—What was her upbringing like? What events have shaped her, influenced her, helped her grow, or frustrated her growth? What sins were hardest to repent of?
- The Present—What are his ongoing struggles? How does he handle daily stresses? Who holds him accountable, and who is accountable for his spiritual growth? What does he fear?
- Hopes—What does she want for herself and her future spouse and family? What does she want for her church? What is her sense of God's mission in the world and her place in it?
- Dreams—What fulfills him? Where does he see himself in the future? What is his vision for your relationship?
- Wounds—What baggage is she carrying? What sins committed against her are still difficult to recover from? Who has hurt her, and how? What still haunts her?

This is why I say the excitement at this stage in the relationship is not simply about attraction and hanging out. It is the excitement about the prospect of beginning a real life together. That decision has not necessarily been made yet, but the potential is there and agreed upon by both parties. Others have confirmed you have potential to be together, and so the conversations you have become less about getting to *know* each other and more about *understanding* each other. This is a period before official engagement but more serious than merely dating. This is the stage I would call "courtship."

THE SERIOUSNESS OF COURTSHIP

Tommy Nelson defined courtship as "the time when you begin to date one person exclusively, frequently, and with the purpose of determining if this is the person with whom you truly want to spend the rest of your life."[1] Joshua Harris said it is "that special season in a romance when a man and woman are seriously weighing the possibility of marriage."[2]

What we see in Song of Solomon 2:8–9 is that Solomon got to know what made this woman tick, and he was fired up about knowing her on this deeper level. The zeal of the initial attraction was still there, but it was fueled by a deeper fire: "My beloved is like a gazelle or a young stag. Behold, there he stands behind our wall, gazing through the windows, looking through the lattice" (v. 9).

Okay, I know this sounds a bit creeper-ish. Guys, don't take the literal reading of this text into your application, all right? This is not a license to stalk a woman. This is a poetic description of something much more appropriate, and it continues in verses 10–13:

> My beloved speaks and says to me:
> "Arise, my love, my beautiful one,
>   and come away,

for behold, the winter is past;
　　the rain is over and gone.
The flowers appear on the earth,
　　the time of singing has come,
and the voice of the turtledove
　　is heard in our land.
The fig tree ripens its figs,
　　and the vines are in blossom;
　　they give forth fragrance.
Arise, my love, my beautiful one,
　　and come away."

First of all, he was not literally peeking through her window to watch her. Instead, what is meant by his standing behind the wall, gazing through the window, and looking through the lattice is that, although his relational position to her was still outside the covenant of marriage, he nevertheless saw beneath the surface. He took stock of her interior life, saw beneath the relational facades, and considered the parts of her she kept hidden.

These verses, then, reveal that she knew he was not running away. Instead, he held out hope to her. "The winter is past; the rain is over" in verse 11 speaks to his optimism about their life together, despite the more difficult things he learned in the deepening of their romance. This is why in verse 14 he said this: "O my dove, in the clefts of the rock, in the crannies of the cliff, let me see your face, let me hear your voice, for your voice is sweet, and your face is lovely."

One reason he is described as peering through the lattice to consider her interior life is that she was still dealing with some insecurity. It is even possible that something came up as they grew in intimacy that caused her to hide. Some kind of information came to light, something in the past reared its head, and it disrupted the romantic euphoria.

But whatever the issue, it didn't dissuade Solomon. He did not pull away; he continued to pursue. She was perhaps still dealing with insecurity, and he was respectful of her feelings so as not to burden her or to pry, but he demonstrated the authenticity of the gospel of grace by refusing to distance himself. He drew nearer.

"Let me see your face," he's saying. "Talk to me. I'm still here. I'm not going to leave. You can tell me anything. I'm still bowled over by you."

Isn't it a deeply satisfying and steadying thing when someone gets a glimpse of our "crazy" and basically says, "I'm not going anywhere"?

This kind of response to less-than-perfect is the greatest indicator that a couple has moved beyond the recreational, curious dating stage and into courtship. It is the first great indicator that they are preparing for a life together; things have gotten substantively serious. If someone is willing at this early stage, before the lifelong covenantal commitment has been made, to cover guilt, shame, hurt, or other difficulty with grace, it is a reasonably hopeful sign that he or she will continue to do so after the commitment is made. And as the relationship moves into the deepening seriousness of courtship, this grace will continue to be tested.

SORTING THROUGH YOUR ISSUES

In the courtship stage, a couple must have conversations about his and her pasts. Back in those days for Lauren and me, we began many conversations with "Here's what you need to know about me …"

"Here's what you need to know about my background …" "Here are some things that happened to me growing up that have left marks on me …" "These are the reasons I act this way …" "These are the reasons certain things bother me …"

We had a lot of questions for each other, and we had a lot of insights about ourselves to share.

This kind of openness obviously creates a risky season in the relationship. But as the relationship progresses—and remember, we've already established safety with each other; we already trust each other—we enter that season when we describe our lives with depth and sincerity reserved only for those who know us most closely.

"Here are my concerns …" "Here's where I'm growing …" "Here's where I'm afraid …" "Here's where I'm struggling …" The conversation is growing in depth, growing in meaning. There is more honesty. There is more risk. There is more willingness to expose our hearts, even though we know that it could still go bad. We're not covenanted yet, and we haven't fully locked in. We haven't said, "Till death do us part." We haven't said, "For better or for worse." But we are moving toward saying those sacred words.

This is why courtship is deeper than dating—because it is dangerous, vulnerable, and awesome all at the same time. We are testing the waters of grace, trying to see if the attraction is evidencing real love, the kind of selfless love the Bible calls married couples to embrace. And precisely because in courtship we show more of our hearts to each other, including the darker parts, courtship can go badly.

My wife and I are dear friends with a single woman who cannot have children. It's just not physiologically possible. Revealing this about herself is part of a conversation in her relationships as they get more serious, and there have been men who walked away because it's something they can't see themselves getting over. As you can imagine, this is extremely hurtful and disappointing to our friend. But she knows she has to bring it up, as risky as the conversation is, as things get more serious.

Obviously, sharing this kind of issue puts a person in a very vulnerable position, but to "save" it until *after* he or she gets married can make both feel even more vulnerable. It can provoke a feeling of betrayal. Issues like this must be addressed before a lifelong commitment is made so that no one feels misled.

And as painful as it can be to have people confront the reality of your issues only to walk away, imagine how confidence building and hope giving it will be when you enter marriage with one who has confronted the reality of your issues and says, "I'm all in. Nothing could stop me from marrying you."

When I was dating Lauren, I had a developing sense of God's calling on my life to serve him in ministry, and it was getting stronger and stronger. In my head, as I considered what this kind of service would entail, I assumed that if we got married, we were going to be broke. And I was thinking God could call us to go overseas. I was thinking that he could send me anywhere to do anything and require me to give up all sorts of things to do it, and I certainly wasn't going to hide any of these thoughts from the one considering spending the rest of her life with me.

We had that conversation at a Chili's restaurant in Longview. It wasn't a very romantic location, of course, but I just put it all out on the table. I said, "Here's where I think the Lord is taking me ..." "Here's what he is calling me into ..." "I don't know how this is going to end, but I need to go. Despite all the uncertainty and the risk, can you come along?"

I'm glad we had that conversation, because I made three transitions before I became the pastor of The Village Church, each of which was at a smaller place and for less money. Lauren knew those kinds of transitions were possible, though, because we had that conversation before we even got married.

Each time I felt the Holy Spirit leading me to consider a smaller ministry and a smaller paycheck, I'd lay it out in front of her and say, "Let's pray about this together. If I sense this is where God wants us to be, can you follow?"

These are the kinds of conversations that you have when you are in courtship. In this stage it's also time to have a conversation about your wounds, about where you've been deeply hurt, whether you were abused or underwent another kind of trauma that makes trust difficult for you. Most of these things will have already started to reveal themselves in your relationship by the time you get to courtship, but now is the time to discuss them. You've probably seen some crazy and wondered what to do with it. It hasn't been enough to make you want to hit eject, but you have thought, *Well,* that *was weird.* Maybe you can't think of an explanation for what happened; maybe the behavior seemed sudden or out of character. In courtship, you've got to sort those things out, though.

Ask questions such as the following: "Where did that come from?" "Why did you do that?" "What were you feeling and thinking when you reacted that way?" "How can I help you?"

Your significant other may retreat in response, so it's important to stay tender, to stay patient, because his or her inclination to open up to you will largely depend on how kind and gracious you are. She may be used to people glimpsing at her emotional dysfunctions and bailing. So it may be difficult for her to trust you won't do the same. Or it could be that nobody has ever even asked her about these things! Maybe she's surprised by the interest and unsettled by it.

Many of us are wounded and don't even realize it. Others of us know we've had moments that marked us, but we haven't fully grasped the damage. Some wounds won't even come out until later, after becoming married. But as much as we are able, before marriage, we must have these conversations.

One thing I learned about myself is this: I desperately wanted to earn the approval of my father. And I found it to be impossible. I just couldn't do it, and that marked me. It embedded in me a terrible insecurity, and that insecurity at times caused me to act like an idiot with Lauren. I'd get frustrated and angry, and it all came out of this "father wound" I was carrying around. If you're familiar with my ministry, you might appreciate my sarcasm and wit, but let me tell you: it's a nightmare when I'm operating out of insecurity. I can cut deep.

In courtship you see each other's wounds, and you also see how you each respond to woundedness. In my life, as things are revealed about me that I wish weren't true, my natural desire is to hide, to not let these things be seen.

In courtship we have conversations about our wounds as best as we understand them. We end up providing insights into ourselves that make our partners either run away or draw nearer. Solomon was a man of God, and he was being called into a relationship of true love for his partner, so he chose the latter.

He was operating under the banner of the kind of love that doesn't leave (see 2:4). The Hebrew word for "love" in Song of

Solomon 2:4 is *ahava*, which describes "love of the will." It's the "I'm not going anywhere" kind of love. It's the love that says, "I've seen the crazy, and I'm going to stick around."

Courtship reveals the presence or lack of *ahava*. Because, as we've said before, isn't everybody on his or her best behavior the first few months of dating? But as we move into courtship, the guard comes down a little. The couple are more relaxed with each other, more at home with each other, so their real selves are coming through.

Solomon peered through the lattice; he's seen her malfunctions. He's made a note to himself: "Okay, that's going to come up again." Right? He thought, *We're going to be dealing with that one for a while.*

But he didn't run.

Look at chapter 2, verse 15: "Catch the foxes for us, the little foxes that spoil the vineyards, for our vineyards are in blossom." The little foxes are representative of their recurring issues.

In courtship, all of a sudden the "little foxes" start coming out, and instead of ignoring them and trying to pretend like they're not there, you work through them together and sort them out. They will ruin the vineyard of your relationship if you don't work together to catch them before they do serious damage.

I'm always worried about people who don't think there are issues to deal with at the levels of courtship and engagement. Have you ever met these people? They are so infatuated with the romance that they forget they're in relationship with a sinner. They especially forget that their partner is in a relationship with a sinner. I'm always telling people at The Village, "Look, marriage is difficult," and I've got about two thousand engaged couples out there in the congregation looking at each other saying, "Not us, baby, not us. It won't be that way for us." Because when you're young and in love, you're kind of oblivious to the storm of dysfunction lying in wait for you.

You've got to start opening up, start being honest with yourself and with each other. Solomon and his woman were honest enough to admit, "Hey, we've got issues." They had a vineyard full of little foxes eating away at their ability to walk in intimacy, eating away at their ability to communicate effectively, eating away at their ability to trust God. But they were committed early on in the courtship stage to catch the foxes before they did too much damage.

Notice the perspective of the statement in Song of Solomon 2:15: "Catch the foxes for *us*." There is an implication of third-party help. They asked for help together, possibly from someone else who loves them. By way of application, I would strongly recommend for every couple in courtship, as you come across the "little foxes," ask for outside help. For some couples, this may mean simply seeking out good premarital counseling. For others, it may mean more intensive gospel-centered counseling individually and as a couple. It certainly means engaging in a discipleship relationship and submitting to spiritual leaders in the church and family.

If you are in a courtship, you're considering uniting with someone for the rest of your life. Why not seek help? Why not ask a wise, godly third party to peek through the lattice too, to consider your interior lives and relationship dynamics and help you navigate with wisdom and godliness through the potential difficulties ahead?

The couple in this Song was doing that. They were prayerfully working through deep heart issues, and part of that meant they were asking for third-party help.

The result for them was continued affirmation of *ahava* love. "My beloved is mine, and I am his; he grazes among the lilies. Until the day breathes and the shadows flee, turn, my beloved, be like a gazelle or a young stag on cleft mountains" (vv. 16–17). Through all of this consideration, he continued to pursue her.

It probably bears mentioning here that when I talk about navigating hard issues and continuing to pursue, I am not recommending (to women in particular) that you seek to be the savior of a violent person. That's not your job. You don't need to put your body on the altar of an abusive person's redemption. Christ has done that.

I know that often this is where third-party help is most important. It unfortunately often takes a third party to counsel victims away from offenders. So I want to be clear about this: If you're in an abusive relationship—whether it's physical or sexual or verbal or spiritual—you need to get out and get help. If you're being victimized, tell the police. Talk to your pastor or elders. Talk to a counselor. But don't think it will get better on its own, and don't think that showing grace means subjecting yourself to abuse. That's not *ahava* love.

Nevertheless, in courtship, *ahava* is affirmed through the joint confrontation and consideration of all the dark spots hidden in the heart. If you don't sense *ahava* is there in your partner for your imperfections, it's a sign that it's probably time to move apart rather than forward. Once in college, I was sitting on my balcony with a dear friend on the night before his wedding, and he said, "Man, this is a mistake."

I said, "Hey, brother, you should cancel this thing."

And he replied with, "Well, her dress cost this, and the dinner cost that."

And I said, "You can't get married because you spent money on a wedding. You should cancel it."

He protested further. "No, we'll work at it."

So I asked him why he said it was a mistake, and he went deep into the dynamics of their relationship and outlined many deficiencies and incompatibilities.

"We don't know what to talk about anymore, we're not connecting on any real level, and I think we've both just thought that if we just get married, these things will work themselves out."

I have to tell you that if in the course of courtship you hit this same ceiling, it is not wise to keep walking together. If, as issues come up, you can't graciously sort through them together and commit to bold love of each other despite them, then you probably shouldn't press on to engagement and marriage.

MOVING TOWARD THE COVENANT

When a relationship deepens, weaknesses come to light, and heart-level issues are raised, many couples pretend those issues aren't there. They turn to something to mask the pain and to help them avoid dealing with the growing seriousness of the relationship. They may medicate with sexual intimacy, getting more and more physical until there's no longer any real conversation at all. Or they may spend most of their time in passive activity—outdoor stuff that involves no opportunity for talking or indoor activities such as watching movies. Medicating away the difficulty and avoiding it provide an illusion of intimacy because a couple is spending time together and remaining physically connected. However, it is a false sense of intimacy because it is outside the biblical boundaries for a couple in this stage. People in this situation aren't really learning about one another anymore; mostly, they're just using each other, pretending to be adults, trying to do adult stuff, including the stuff that comes with the privilege of the marriage covenant without actually making the commitment and doing the real work of a relationship. The results are absolutely devastating.

Solomon and the Shulammite woman realized this is a real danger. They realized, "Hey, we've got issues we need to work through. Before we're free to turn on the physical side of our relationship, let's pull back on the reins." They wanted to make sure growth was in place so they didn't wind up using and hurting one another.

The trajectory they followed was sound for them, and it remains spiritually and therefore relationally sound for us today. They respected each other, cared for each other, spent time getting to know each other, and ministered to one another. They sought outside counsel. They were submissive to God's Word. When difficult things came up, they persevered through them and committed to bring grace at each place of tenderness.

So the relationship kept moving forward, and the second chapter of the Song of Solomon ends like this: "My beloved is mine, and I am his; he grazes among the lilies. Until the day breathes and the shadows flee, turn, my beloved, be like a gazelle or a young stag on cleft mountains" (vv. 16–17).

Here's what happened: Specifically on her part, there was deepening trust for Solomon because as issues arose, he didn't run but instead said, "Let's deal with them." He didn't medicate; he didn't try to take advantage of her when she felt weak and vulnerable. They slowed things down, they worked through their issues, and look how she responded:

> On my bed by night
> I sought him whom my soul loves;
>> I sought him, but found him not.
> I will rise now and go about the city,
>> in the streets and in the squares;
> I will seek him whom my soul loves.
>> I sought him, but found him not.
> The watchmen found me
>> as they went about in the city.
> "Have you seen him whom my soul loves?"
> Scarcely had I passed them
>> when I found him whom my soul loves.
> I held him, and would not let him go
>> until I had brought him into my mother's
>>> house,
>> and into the chamber of her who conceived
>>> me. (3:1–4)

Her desire for him continued to be kindled. She longed to be with him and dreamed of him. And then? She brought him home to meet Mom. "I … would not let him go until I had brought him into my mother's house."

Ideally, even for adult-aged couples living on their own, as the relationship becomes more serious, they should meet each other's parents, if possible. In this stage of courtship, time with each other's parents has a greater seriousness. Mom and Dad are considering the inclusion of a new son or daughter to the family. When you marry someone, you are joining his or her family, so beginning to experience family life together becomes more important.

This is a necessary step in courtship, and it's something that must be ongoing, assuming you don't live so far away that it's impossible. Time with family is also about more than getting to know each other. On the role of parents in courtship, John Thomas wrote:

> [It's] much more than just saying, "We bless this relationship." It's offering guidance, within proper boundaries, and modeling the kind of relationship you'd like to see your children experience. It's helping them avoid the pitfalls you have experienced or seen others experience. It's cheering them on and helping them gain confidence as they navigate new waters.
>
> As for specifics, think about what you wish someone had asked you, now that you have the benefit of hindsight. Ask him some questions that get him thinking, like, "What is it about our daughter that attracts you to her? What are some of the qualities you admire most about her? What do you hope to accomplish or discover during the courtship season? What steps will you take to seek God's guidance through this season? What are the things you are looking for to confirm that she is who you want to spend the rest of your life with? How will you be held accountable for purity during this season?"

His answers to those thought-provoking questions should give you a fairly good idea of his seriousness, and at the very least it will get him thinking about things that matter. And yes, you should make sure your daughter is on board, and that she too is being asked some of the same questions.[3]

In courtship, a couple are moving more and more toward entering the covenant of marriage, even if they are not engaged yet. In a weird way, they are perhaps "engaged to be engaged." In any event, the idea of marriage becomes a growing reality ahead of them, and because biblically speaking, marriage is a covenant between two people in the grace of God in Christ, it necessarily has the communal context of church and family. The reason Christians get married "before the church" is not to give a religious appearance to the ceremony but because Christians hold the marriage covenant in the context of the community of the body of Christ. Seeking the support and counsel of family is an extension of this.

I know this kind of family involvement can be difficult for all kinds of reasons, not the least of which may be because many young Christian couples come from non-Christian families. But as much as you are able, ground your marriage in the greater fabric of family life and legacy because it can strengthen your relationship, increase your wisdom, and enhance the sense that you are part of something greater than yourselves.

The church context is also important. A couple seeking to do married life apart from the teaching, discipleship, community, and grace of a local church is making things much harder than they have to be. Yes, your relationship is yours. You are not going to be married to anyone but your future spouse. But your marriage does not exist in a vacuum. Because marriage is meant to reflect the great sacrificial and sanctifying love Christ has for his church, it makes sense to connect your married life to a local Christian congregation.

When a couple are making an effort to take these steps in courtship, they are making it more obvious that they are ready to enter the covenant of marriage.

DEALING (STILL) WITH GROWING SEXUAL DESIRE

After our gal has brought Solomon home to meet Mom, we come to this refrain: "I adjure you, O daughters of Jerusalem, by the gazelles or the does of the field, that you not stir up or awaken love until it pleases" (3:5).

Now, that sounds very familiar, doesn't it? We've heard this before. Twice, as this relationship grew to another level, this young woman pleaded for things not to get overly physical.

We're going to keep coming back to this because the reality of sexuality is all over the Song of Solomon. Some commentators have noted that the Song is primarily a manual to sexual intimacy. While their emphasis may be a little heavy, they aren't necessarily misreading the sexual resonance throughout the entire song.

This recurring refrain—"do not awaken love until it pleases" (or "until it's time")—is a reminder that for our sexually interested couple, only the covenant of marriage will sanctify sexual consummation.

If you are in a growing romantic relationship, you should read this text as directly applicable to you. The woman is pleading with *you*. Don't let your relationship get too physical.

When you remove the relational element of sex—even if you're married—and sex becomes just physical, what you've done is under-cut the ability to create and nurture genuine, legitimate intimacy. Sex becomes this weird pill you can take that makes you *feel* intimate with one another but actually facilitates the opposite of intimacy.

Have you ever wondered why every magazine in the grocery store checkout line has an article on sex that always has something to do with technique?

"Nine Ways to Be a Better Lover," "Seven Spots She Wishes You Would Touch"—that kind of thing. Why are the magazines always pushing technique? Well, if you're having sex with different men or women and it doesn't bring you lasting joy or fulfillment, the only hope you have for intimacy and sexual fulfillment is to improve your technique. "And maybe, just maybe," the magazines implicitly promise, "if you become a better lover, then this aching in your soul will go away. Maybe if you become a better lover, you'll be satisfied."

Incidentally, this is why porn is unbelievably devastating. It holds out an ever-increasing promise of satisfaction while simultane-ously, gradually *removing* the ability to be intimate. Porn makes sex purely physical, and when it becomes purely physical, it loses the glory God has designed it to have. You lose that glory even in mar-riage when sex becomes purely about the physical act of intercourse, and you certainly forfeit this glory when you engage in sex outside of marriage. Sex outside of marriage is deliberate disobedience of God's commands, which are for your good, and therefore it is a deliberate forfeiture of your own spiritual well-being, as well as your own *sexual* well-being!

The repeated warning in Song of Solomon 3:5 is well-timed, because the good desire for physical intimacy will likely only grow as a couple approaches marriage. Even as a couple nears the commitment, the temptation can become greater to begin "bending" some rules, assuming that the intention to commit authorizes some things and blurs some lines. The pull toward physical intimacy will feel almost overpowering at the courtship stage, and the lie that "We are going to get married anyway" will be one that must be addressed and confessed often.

This temptation is one that anyone who has been married and spent a considerable time engaged is familiar with. Maybe they suppressed it, maybe they fought it, but it certainly came up. The longer the engagement lasts, or the closer the wedding day comes, the greater the temptation becomes. "Hey, we're only two weeks out. What's two weeks?" But this seemingly compelling logic is exactly what Solomon's woman "adjures" (or "pleads with") us to reject. She wouldn't be pleading if the temptation was weak.

It's important for us to understand that when the Bible says to "keep waiting," it's not trying to take anything from us. God's not trying to rob you of an experience but rather lead you into a greater one, and the arguments of our culture are absurd. For instance:

"Well, how will you know if you're sexually compatible?"
Because I'm a man and she's a woman.

"How do you know that you're going to work out well together?"

Well, we don't! That's the importance of the covenant of grace. We'll figure it out. We are making the promise to figure it out with God's help, whatever happens.

Before we make the vow before God, we don't want to derail the good pleasure God has designed for us. We don't want to get in his way. He's leading us toward a greater reality than sexual gratification, wooing us into what will be best for our joy and for his glory.

So, please, don't think that God is sexually repressed. Wait till we get to the fourth chapter of Solomon's Song! We'll cover that portion of the text more closely in the fifth chapter of this book, but there's no way a reasonable person could read the Song of Solomon and come away thinking that God is a prude or that his Word is somehow embarrassed by sex.

The world is certainly not embarrassed by its sexual activity, even though it should be. God, who designed the act of sexual intercourse and wired us to be sexual beings, should absolutely not be. He has every right to explain all we need to know in his Word to find the kind of sexual satisfaction that will bring us joy and him glory. That kind of sexual satisfaction is reserved for a man and woman in the covenant of marriage as a recurring consummation and "ratifying" of their union. That is the godly, wise way to live out our sexuality.

But the biblical way of wisdom is not the way most of us live our lives. If you're a single person reading this book, statistically speaking, you are not a virgin. It's quite likely that you have, in the words of Solomon's Song but contrary to its admonition, "awakened love before its time."

Rules of behavior are not the only kind of wisdom God gives us in his Word, nor are they even the best kind, especially if 2 Corinthians

3:9 is to be believed. The gospel is better than the law, and for those who have engaged in sexual sin, there is much gospel to be had.

There are two stories in particular in the Bible that radically reorient how we see and understand who God is and what God has done for us in Jesus Christ. Both stories involve sexually promiscuous women.

The first is about a woman caught in adultery. An angry, religious mob grabbed this poor, naked woman—leaving the man behind, for reasons probably having to do with misogyny and prejudice—and dragged her to the feet of Jesus, hoping to catch him in a tricky situation. They said to him, "The Law says that this woman caught in the act of adultery should be stoned to death. What do you say?"

Just imagine for a moment that God sent an angry mob after you when you engaged in sexual sin. Imagine the shame of being busted publicly in your sin, of being exposed spiritually and *physically*, of being dragged naked in front of a crowd of hateful people yelling at you and accusing you, taunting you, teasing you. Can you feel the fear? The vulnerability? Can you feel the hopelessness? The despair?

Imagine they have thrown you at the feet of a highly respected righteous man. And the law of the land is that the penalty for your sin is death.

The storm of emotion inside this woman must have been suffocating. Regret, fear, shame, desperation, shock—all at once.

The Bible, in John 8, says that Jesus bent down and started to draw with his finger in the dirt. I don't know why, but I've always thought it's the coolest thing ever. Nobody knows what he wrote in the ground, but after he doodled in the sand, Jesus stood and said, "Let the one who is without sin cast the first stone."

From oldest to youngest, the accusers dropped their rocks and walked away. But that's not the part that gets me. The part that gets me is when Jesus walked over to the woman, took her face in his hands, maybe wiped away all her tears and dirt and shame—and if there were any eyes she didn't want to look into, they would be the eyes of Jesus, the most holy man who ever lived—and said to her, "Where are your accusers, woman? Has no one condemned you?"

She replied, "No one."

And the holy king of Israel replied, "Neither do I. Go and sin no more."

After reading this, can you doubt there is abundant grace for the most ashamed of sinners?

In another encounter, Jesus was walking through Samaria when he stopped at Jacob's well at noon. A woman approached the well, and what's interesting is that this was not a common time of day for women to come to the well. Most came early in the morning or later in the evening to avoid the heat, but this woman came in the heat of midday. It is suspected by most scholars that she wanted to avoid people. Maybe she was carrying shame and didn't want to deal with scolding looks and turned-up noses from other women.

In the dialogue that ensued between this woman and Jesus, he revealed that she was married multiple times and the man who she was living with at the time was not her husband. It appears to be kind of a "sex for rent" arrangement. Jesus began the conversation with the topic of worship, but through that, Jesus revealed to her the reality of his kingship. Part of this reality, part of the breaking in of God's kingdom through him as Messiah, was the invitation he gave to her: "I want to give you water so that you'll never thirst again" (see John 4).

We have to wrap our minds around the fact that this woman had been treated very cheaply, and as a result, she treated herself very cheaply. And then a Jewish man, who should have been the most judgmental toward her, offered her eternally satisfying refreshment.

I've been a pastor long enough to know the effects of sexual abuse. I know that women don't become strippers or prostitutes because they aspired to these careers as little girls. It's a long, dark road that leads women into circumstances like these. It is often the result of desperate choices made in the wake of abuse and oppression. They've been taken advantage of by people they trusted. Any woman who is trying to avoid prying eyes and mocking lips also has the opportunity to stand before the sinless Messiah, the one who will judge righteously. And Jesus's response to her will not be, "Clean yourself up." Or, "Aren't you ashamed of yourself?"

It will be, "I want to give you water so that you'll never thirst again."

To the woman at the well, Jesus was basically saying, "You are trying to quench your thirst with these men. This desperate thirst you have coming out of the emotional and spiritual desert of your life ... I want to give you water that quenches that thirst forever." Christ's response to her was sorrowful, broken, tender, and redemptive.

So if you're in a place of having been made to feel shameful, you should know there is good news. You don't have to surrender to shame. You don't have to be owned by regret. You don't have to live forever under a dark cloud of guilt. The holy God of the universe who has condemned your sin and promised wrath for the unrepentant workers of disobedience offers you—freely, abundantly, mightily—total and absolute forgiveness, *forever*. To all who trust in

Jesus Christ for salvation, his righteousness becomes theirs, his holiness becomes theirs, his security in the Father becomes theirs. And if you are repentant and believe in him, his grace is yours.

Christ has brought about the redemption of our past and a recognition that he is able to make all things new. So what can happen right now, even as you read this book, is that by his grace you can lay down your sin, ask for his forgiveness, and walk away completely blameless (see Col. 1:22; Jude 1:24).

This is possible even if you're in the midst of sexual sin right now. Maybe it is God's will for you to be married, and your relationship has great potential for godliness, but it is marred by physical intimacy before its time. You can both repent.

Men, you should lead the way by apologizing to your woman, asking for her forgiveness and promising to pursue her heart in godly ways. It's never too late to repent and start anew by God's grace.

You must believe that God is not holding out on you, that he isn't withholding sex from you to make you miserable. He has something greater in store for you. And if you as a couple can trust him together and believe in the wisdom of his Word and the godly counsel of his servants in the church, your relationship will go to better places than sexual intimacy can take you.

If you are willing to repent in this area and cling to the gospel with desperate abandon in order to honor each other and work toward each other's sanctification, the day of marriage will be that much sweeter.

CHAPTER FOUR

WEDDING BELLS

One of the greatest privileges I have as a pastor is officiating wedding ceremonies. It is absolutely one of my favorite things to do. There's a special kind of energy present on a wedding day. It's the rare occasion when all the people a couple loves are gathered in one room together. The people who have most influenced and shaped the couple's lives have all assembled to celebrate this love that God has brought into their lives.

And while I enjoy all the aesthetic beauty that is produced on a wedding day—from the dresses to the decorations, from the desserts to the dance floor—I am most interested at weddings in the beauty underneath all the beauty we're seeing. So at every wedding I've ever officiated, I have said these words at some point in the ceremony:

> All of this is beautiful today: the candles and
> the dresses, the tuxes and the flowers. But there

is something roaring underneath it all. And if we miss it, then today's occasion will be shallow. Because the real intent behind all of this is that we might know and grasp God's love for us, his pursuit of us, his romance of us, despite being a people who prefer what was created rather than our Creator.

What I'm trying to do at a wedding ceremony is highlight the reality grounding the reality. If we don't make the spiritual reality the main point, we're actually going to *miss* the point. Because all the hard work that goes into the wedding day fades away. The cake gets eaten. The clothing goes back to the rental shop. The dress is stored away. The decorations are trashed or recycled. The flowers wilt. The reality of the marriage must remain long after the reality of the wedding has faded.

When I officiate, I draw attention to Ephesians 5:22–33, which explains what's going on when a man pursues a woman and they enter into a covenant relationship together. In light of Paul's words there (and elsewhere) on marriage, the covenantal union of a man and a woman is a shadow of God's pursuing love and affection for his bride, the church. And what we see in a wedding ceremony is a shadow of God's loving, merciful pursuit of us in Christ.

Therefore, it's important to give God so much glory on the wedding day, to give him credit for the entire romance from beginning to end. We want to rejoice in this fact that that "Day of Epiphany" occurred in the groom's heart. Something clicked, and he wanted a woman. Yes, of course that's a biological impulse, but it's a biological impulse because God invented human biology. The man's desire for a bride exists to show us that God in Christ desired a people.

At a wedding we celebrate that a woman's affections were won by this man. Similarly, we are celebrating that Christ wooed his people away from their idols, away from their self-reliance, and into his tender and loving care.

So when those doors swing open and all the people stand and gaze upon the bride in her dazzling wedding gown, they traditionally see her arrayed in white as a representation of her virginal purity. The bride may or may not actually be a virgin, but the white dress is a reminder that every sinner who comes to the Savior is made spotless before his presence.

The couple make vows to each other because God has not just called them to profess romantic love to one another but to profess a particular *kind* of love, the kind that endures, that sticks, that commits.

The man promises to lead and sacrifice. The woman promises to trust and respect. Vows patterned this way reflect the truth of the gospel.

If the gospel of Jesus Christ is not at the center of a wedding ceremony, it is likely not going to be at the center of the marriage. This would be a grave mistake, however, as marriage itself is designed to be a great reflector of that gospel.

CONTRACT VERSUS COVENANT

Before we return to the Song of Solomon, I want us to take a look at Ephesians 5:22–33. This passage informs what we are seeing when a man pursues a woman and enters into a covenant relationship with her. Marriage is a picture—although an imperfect one—of Christ and the church.

> Wives, submit to your own husbands, as to the Lord. For the husband is the head of the wife even as Christ is the head of the church, his body, and is himself its Savior. Now as the church submits to Christ, so also wives should submit in everything to their husbands.
>
> Husbands, love your wives, as Christ loved the church and gave himself up for her, that he might sanctify her, having cleansed her by the washing of water with the word, so that he might present the church to himself in splendor, without spot or wrinkle or any such thing, that she might be holy and without blemish. In the same way husbands should love their wives as their own bodies. He who loves his wife loves himself. For no one ever hated his own flesh, but nourishes and cherishes it, just as Christ does the church, because we are members of his body. "Therefore a man shall leave his father and mother and hold fast to his wife, and the two shall become one flesh." This mystery is profound, and I am saying that it refers to Christ and the church. However, let each one of you love his wife as himself, and let the wife see that she respects her husband.

Paul's mention of wifely submission and husbandly sacrifice—particularly the submission stuff!—is not exactly popular today. But one reason it is there in the biblical prescription for marriage relationships is precisely because it cuts against the grain of our flesh. Apart from a profound work of the Spirit, women do not want to submit to their husbands. And apart from a profound work of the Spirit, men do not want to sacrifice for their wives. So we see how the biblical pattern for the marital dynamic requires the grace of God. It is another way marriages are meant to reflect the gospel, as husbands and wives deny themselves, take up their crosses, and follow Christ into *his* way of loving their spouses.

It is certainly not the world's way. The way our culture tends to depict the working marriage relationship resembles less the covenant of grace and more a business arrangement.

If you're over the age of sixteen, it's likely that much of your life is dictated and directed by the contracts you have agreed to. For example, if you have a cell phone, you entered into a contract with your mobile carrier. If you make car payments, the contract is binding on you until you've paid it all off. If you own a house, you signed a mortgage. If you are renting a home, you signed a lease. Insurance, cable television—most anything you pay bills for—involve entering into a contractual agreement. Even using Wi-Fi in certain public locations involves agreeing to their terms of service. Everywhere you turn, there's a contract to sign. We live in a contract culture.

At a fundamental level, a contract is an agreement between two parties arranging an exchange of goods or services. One party agrees to provide something for the other in exchange for something else.

For most of our contracts, that something else is money. It's all very businesslike, which is why it's called a contract. It's not relational.

And here's what that means: if either party interrupts the reciprocity—if one party refuses to supply the service or the other refuses to supply the payment—then the contract is broken and must be either renegotiated or voided altogether.

For instance, if you pick up your cell phone and it doesn't work, after you have a total meltdown because you can't check Facebook, you find another way to contact your carrier and complain. You're paying good money; why can't they provide a reliable service? Alternatively, if you stop paying your bill, after they've added sufficient late fees and sent you delinquency notices, they'll just cut off your service. According to the contract, if one party fails to live up to its end of the arrangement, the contract is broken and the arrangement is altered.

Now, how does this compare when people talk about the "marriage contract"? Sometimes when people talk about marriage, they talk about partnership in a good, biblical way. But sometimes when they say marriage is a partnership, they make it sound like a business arrangement. "You need to give fifty-fifty," they might say.

But this is terrible advice. It is worldly advice. It does not reflect the reality of marriage, which is a reflection of the unique reality of the gospel. After all, Jesus Christ did not say to sinners in need of redemption, "Meet me halfway. Let's go fifty-fifty on this deal."

No, marriage is not contractual; it is covenantal.

At the wedding ceremony, then, we have to be careful come vow time. The bride and groom turn away from the minister, face each other, and make profound promises. The vows are their public profession of commitment to one another. They announce in their vows before many witnesses *what they mean to do*.

The vows must never be contractual. Never, ever, ever. If the vows were explicitly contractual, we'd probably all gasp and realize the marriage is headed for trouble. We would certainly recognize something was wrong if the couple turned to each other and the bride said, "Look, I'm in this thing as long as you mow the lawn," or if the groom said, "Well, I'll stick around so long as you keep the dishes clean and the laundry done."

If I heard vows like that, I'd retrieve my gift from the pile and head home. I'd be thinking, *There's no way they're gonna pawn this thing when their marriage crashes and burns in a few months.*

If we heard vows like that, we'd know right away that the couple was thinking contractually. While hardly any couples exchange vows with conditions like that, way too many couples treat their vows like that in their hearts. Since we are sinners, our natural responses in relationships usually hinge on what might be gained. We tend to turn all our relationships into contractual arrangements of some kind. We'll sacrifice for our spouse if she deserves it. We'll submit to our spouse if he agrees with us. We'll serve our spouse if she'll serve us in return. But these kinds of thoughts bear no resemblance to the gracious covenant God makes with us.

In a covenant, we don't barter around services. We're not trying to get under a tax shelter. We're entering into a relationship in such a way that we give ourselves to one another. Vows aren't contractual. They're covenantal. They sound like the traditional promises: "For better or for worse. For richer or for poorer. In sickness and in health. Till death do us part." That's covenantal language.

In the covenant of marriage, husband and wife give themselves to each other. It's not fifty-fifty; it's one hundred–one hundred. At any given time either spouse won't have 100 percent to give, but this does not diminish the other's commitment because they are not in a contract but a covenant. As in the covenant of grace initiated by God to save sinners, one party can give 100 percent even if the other gives nothing.

In a gospel-centered marriage, you give yourself to your spouse regardless of the goods or the services because that's what true love is and because that's what glorifies God.

If everything goes great and you find out as you start your life together that the marriage is exactly what you expected, you're in. But if you're like every other normal human being and things get a little problematic, and you find out you married a sinner who's got some crazy he or she was hiding away, *you're still in.*

This is why biblical marriage is so serious—and why divorce is so serious. Ephesians 5 helps us see the weight of the glory of the gospel. Submission is weighty. Sacrifice is weighty. They are weighty like the good news of Jesus Christ is weighty. They are as heavy as the cross.

And in forgiving and loving our sinful spouse, we begin to understand on a much smaller scale what it meant for our holy God to forgive and redeem us.

God's relationship to the church is not contractual; it's covenantal. And what's mind-blowing about God's covenantal love toward the church is that God fulfills the obligations of both parties! God has put on my life the command that I am to love my wife, Lauren, as Christ loved the church. That is God's command on my life—regardless of whether or not she reciprocates that love. I don't love her as Christ loved the church in order to get something from her; I love her that way because that is what God has commanded me to do, and that's the way he has loved me.

When there *is* reciprocity—when she receives my love, and when she returns that love—it's easier to love her, of course. But there is a beauty even in loving without response because that kind of love is truly selfless. When we love with no expectation or promise of reciprocity, we know what it means to sacrifice and deny ourselves in ways we wouldn't otherwise. And even in happy, healthy marriages, there will be ample opportunities for this kind of one-way grace. In fact, the ample presence of one-way grace is a sign of a happy, healthy marriage!

As in the gospel, in marriage we may also begin to see that the grace that attracts us will sustain us. In God's covenant with his people, he doesn't just initiate the covenant in grace; he also enables our ability to respond rightly to the covenant he's initiated.

WHAT GOD HAS JOINED TOGETHER

The ceremonial fanfare has begun. The flowers are scattered along the aisle, and the wedding march announces the congregational doors have been thrown open, revealing the bride in her splendor, ready to be presented. And this vision is a glimpse into how the Lord sees his own.

This is how Jesus sees his bride: spotless and blameless. He delights in her; he rejoices in her. For the wedding ceremony to have a lasting joy long after the reception, this delight and rejoicing must remain into the days when the virginal sheen is gone.

One of the things a married couple must be completely in tune with is God's love for us made manifest in sending Jesus to marry the bride. His love has been an initiating love; his love has been a pursuing love; his love has been a romantic love. But his love has also been a missional love, in that it is commissioned by the Father. The marriage of Christ and his bride is a covenant predestined, designed, and inaugurated by the Father. It is a work of God.

Likewise, for marital love to endure, it must not be sourced in the feelings of husband and wife, which wax and wane and differ—not just year to year, but day to day. Love must be seeded in the eternal purposes of God. A covenantal marriage is God's handiwork.

Returning to the Song of Solomon, look at chapter 3, verse 6: "What is that coming up from the wilderness like columns of smoke, perfumed with myrrh and frankincense, with all the fragrant powders of a merchant?"

The couple celebrated that God was involved in bringing the two of them together. The imagery here is meant to be reminiscent of the children of Israel in the wilderness. Do you remember how they were guided through the wilderness? It was by pillars of smoke during the day (see Exod. 13:21–22). Just as God led the children of Israel out of slavery and into freedom, so Solomon and his bride were led by God away from self-reliance and into the liberating grace of covenantal union.

We have to be careful with this line of thinking, though. While I am a passionate believer that God is at work in space and time, and that he is sovereign over all things, I have never been particularly convinced by the idea that there's a "one" for you. I just see no reason to agree with the worldly romantic notion that every person has just

WEDDING BELLS / 107

one "soul mate" out there waiting for him or her. In fact, I find that idea to be anticovenantal, contrary to grace. It forces prospective spouses into a routine of measuring up, of being investigated or even interrogated rather than considered. It turns the search for a godly spouse into an audition to be the one who "completes" you. Do you see the subtle pride at work there, the arrogance? Instead of appropriately considering the character of a potential spouse, the romantic relationship becomes about scrutinizing every potential spouse to see if he or she is "the one" for you, as if you are the be-all and end-all.

No spouse can complete you. Don't look for a spouse to do what only Jesus can.

Even if it were true that there is one person out there for you, isn't it possible that someone messed up the whole relationship order, like, fifty years ago? I mean, if just one person married the wrong spouse back in the day, do the math—the whole system's broken like a domino effect of incompleteness.

So quit looking for "the one." You have a better chance of finding an Oompa Loompa riding a unicorn, fighting Bigfoot.

I do know that God is sovereign over all things. I do believe he is at work in space and time. I know this because when I was in college leading a rather large Bible study, I was often put in the uncomfortable position of Christian girls becoming interested in me—except they weren't really interested in the real me, but rather in whatever image they had of me because of my influence and position. They got pretty good at working the image too, doing whatever they thought it was I needed to see in a godly girl.

In a Christian college there are also a lot of girls hoping to meet and marry someone in ministry. They want to marry a pastor (I think that's because they don't quite understand what we do). This desire is built around so many assumptions.

It was in the midst of all this that I met Lauren. As I said before, we lived about five hours away from each other. She knew I led a Bible study, but she wasn't thinking I taught a thousand people—she was thinking I had a few guys over to my apartment for fellowship and a little teaching. Right off the bat, the image projection, the interest being based on an idea or aspiration, just didn't exist with Lauren. She didn't know anything about the impressive veneer or the reputation. She was interested in *me*.

I found that wildly attractive.

I could clearly see God at work in that. I could have easily been swayed by the efforts of the other girls to impress me. I could have been swayed by their claims to be impressed *by* me. I know that God was at work because he brought me into this relationship with a godly woman who wasn't putting forth an image. And I was very excited by the reality that someone wanted to get to know me—not me the preacher, not me the speaker, just me.

For more than a year, Lauren's and my relationship was long-distance, conducted almost entirely on the phone aside from my weekend visits. It wasn't until later that she showed up where I taught and said, "Wow." But I knew she loved me before she saw that stuff, so I could trust her.

I will give you this credit on the idea of "the one." I know there is a "one" for me. Her name is Lauren. She was Lauren Walker; now she's Lauren Chandler. And here's how I know she's "the one": she said yes.

I'm wearing a ring and she's wearing a ring and we made vows to one another. Because God is at work in space and time, because he is sovereign over all things, we don't get into conflict or difficult times and wonder if we missed out on "the one." We trust in God and realize that "the one" is the one you're in covenant with.

The idea of "the one" can undercut the grace God gives for marriage to be a reflection of the gospel because it can cause us to doubt whether this sinner we married is actually that one. We doubt this especially when he or she doesn't seem to be "completing" us very well, when we don't feel especially fulfilled in our marriage. When we begin to give in to our own self-interests, when we cave to lustful temptations, or when we just flat out get bored or irritated, our thoughts often turn away from giving grace to our spouse and toward wondering if the reason we've got all this trouble is because we didn't marry the right person.

So that kind of thinking disgraces marriage because marriage is something God does through us. It is why many wedding ceremonies conclude with this warning, straight from the mouth of Jesus: "What therefore God has joined together, let not man separate" (Mark 10:9). Of course, these words are often said in a perfunctory way, but they speak to the deep spiritual reality of marriage: it is something God has done. To think of it as anything less is to diminish it.

Solomon and the Shulammite woman, then, commenced their nuptials with a celebration of God's authorship of covenantal grace and therefore God's authorship of their marriage. By sending up perfumed smoke, they were saying, "Look at how God has worked to bring us together! Look at what we have overcome." Their wedding was a celebration of all that God had accomplished to lead them to that moment.

As Song of Solomon 3 progresses, we see another important aspect of their wedding ceremony, another contextual facet to their relationship that reflects a greater reality. They stood in front of friends and family members who served not only as witnesses to their covenant but also as supporters of it.

THE COMMUNITY REJOICES

Can we agree that it's not a good sign if there are disgruntled or otherwise disapproving family members at the wedding? Sometimes weddings get complicated by influential people in one of the families who wish to undermine the marriage from day one. There used to be the traditional call somewhere near the beginning of a wedding ceremony where the minister would say, "If anyone has cause to object to this union, speak now or forever hold your peace." They don't say that too much anymore, and I wonder if it's because too many people were speaking up and rocking the boat.

This was not the case at Solomon's wedding.

> Behold, it is the litter of Solomon!
> Around it are sixty mighty men,
>   some of the mighty men of Israel,
> all of them wearing swords
>   and expert in war,
> each with his sword at his thigh,
>   against terror by night. (3:7–8)

Who were these guys? The groomsmen!

This was an epic wedding. There were 60 groomsmen; they were carrying swords, and they would be paired up with 60 bridesmaids who were all decked out in beautiful dresses. Solomon and his bride had 120 people proceed up and down that aisle. Their wedding was stacked with people celebrating and supporting them, loaded with friends and colleagues adorning them in their ceremonial splendor. It was a beautiful sight, no doubt, but it was indicative of more than just the pomp and circumstance of a royal wedding.

Remember that godly counsel? Remember those friends who celebrated? They were all there and were thrilled to be there.

One of the things I earnestly hope for and love to see in a Christian wedding is when the groomsmen present are men who have walked alongside the groom as godly friends. They have prayed for him, encouraged him as he fought for purity, and stood with him as he desired to be the man God would have him be to shepherd his bride's heart. They have been fighting the fight with him. This is why one of my favorite moments before a wedding is getting to go hang out with the groomsmen before the ceremony and hear one of them say, "Let's pray." I get to watch those young men lay their hands on their brother and plead with the Lord concerning his marriage. My hope and expectation is that the bridesmaids are doing the same.

What we see on Solomon's wedding day is a celebration of what God has done, not just through the couple but through everyone involved in their lives. In fact, Song of Solomon 3:11 gives us insight into this reality: "Go out, O daughters of Zion, and look upon King Solomon, with the crown with which his mother crowned him on the day of his wedding, on the day of the gladness of his heart."

As a parent, I can certainly relate to this text. Solomon's mama was rejoicing.

This is a big deal. It is not an easy thing for mamas to move to the second chair. It's so difficult that the Bible issues an edict that a son must leave his mother and father and cleave to his wife. Very often moms of boys don't want to become the second woman in their boy's life. So one of the signs that dating and courtship have occurred in a way that is right and respectful is that mom is *for* this.

Solomon's mother watched this woman love her son. She watched this woman engage her son's heart. She saw the joy brought into her baby boy's life by this woman. And she was happy for them. She was proud of her daughter-in-law. She joyfully handed over the feminine care of her boy to his wife.

Should we even get started on daddies and little girls? My role as the father of two daughters is to get them ready to not need me, then to hand them off to men who will show them the care and love of Christ, who will nurture their souls as I have had the privilege to do from the second they breathed their first breath right up until I walk them down that aisle. I know that's my job. I don't think it's going to be easy.

I have a dear friend in Houston whose youngest daughter got married, and when the young man approached my friend to ask for his daughter's hand in marriage, my friend said, "Let's talk. Do you know what you're asking me?"

"Yeah," the kid said, "I know what I'm asking. I'm asking if I can marry your daughter."

"Okay," my friend replied. "Tell me what you think that means. For example, you realize what I've done for her the first twenty-four years of her life, right? I've been that place where she can come and cry. I've been that place where she can be honest about struggles. I've been the one who's spoken the gospel into her heart. I've been her biggest cheerleader, an expert on her strengths, tenderly engaging her weak spots. Are you telling me you're ready to do that? Because if you're telling me you're ready to do that, I'll say yes. If you're not ready to do that, then I'm telling you no."

For a dad to say yes, for a dad to rejoice in his daughter's wedding day, for a daddy to walk his little girl down the aisle—this little girl he held as a baby, burped and paddled and taught and cheered and supported and prayed for—is a monumental thing. For him to rejoice in handing her over to a younger (usually), more foolish man, entrusting the deep parts of her soul to a guy who knows little about marriage except that he wants to be in one, is not easy.

When dating and courtship occur as they should, then the wedding day will be filled with rejoicing. There will be a celebration that God was involved. There will be rejoicing by the friends and the family members who are there, including Mom and Dad.

At this point in the Song, all the community involvement, especially of the church, culminated in a crescendo of joy for the couple and worship of God. The reputations of Solomon and his bride were complimented by their community. They had their fears consoled by their community. They had their hearts counseled by their community. So the community gathered to rest from this work and begin new work—witnessing the couple's union and pledging to support them in the new stage of the relationship, the enduring covenant of marriage.

THE HUSBAND'S SACRIFICIAL LEAD

If we go back to that very first covenantal union in Genesis 3 and see where it all went wrong, we notice something peculiar and important about the relational breakdown between Adam and Eve.

> But the serpent said to the woman, "You will not surely die. For God knows that when you eat of it your eyes will be opened, and you will be like God, knowing good and evil." So when the woman saw that the tree was good for food, and that it was a delight to the eyes, and that the tree was to be desired to make one wise, she took of its fruit and ate, and she also gave some to her husband who was with her, and he ate. (vv. 4–6)

Did you catch that? Look at that last verse. Eve "also gave some to her husband *who was with her.*" While the serpent was engaging Eve, tempting her to disbelieve God and disobey his commandments, Adam apparently just stood there, mutely witnessing the whole scene.

There is something extremely important to be seen here because it sets up the relational breakdown that has occurred in almost every marriage since this first one: passivity. On Solomon's wedding day we receive a vision meant to reflect the groom's commitment to resist the Adamic curse. Our godly groom was determined to reject the passivity so prevalent among men in the marriage relationship.

King Solomon made himself a carriage
    from the wood of Lebanon.
He made its posts of silver,
    its back of gold, its seat of purple;
its interior was inlaid with love
    by the daughters of Jerusalem. (vv. 9–10)

Now, what occurred on their wedding day after the visions of the beautiful bride and the community rejoicing was a vision of the strength of Solomon. Witnesses to the ceremony marveled at his power. They saw that he was strong, broad, regal, and dignified.

This may sound really odd to you, but it is significant for the very reason that the Bible continues to tell us that the root sin plaguing fallen masculinity is the sin of passivity. It can be seen over and over again, walking forward from Genesis 3, whether it's Abraham lying about his wife or Moses making excuses in reply to God's call or Noah's slump into drunken laziness after the flood … the list goes on and on. Pick a man who stumbles and falls in incredible ways, and his sins always have a root in some fundamental passivity. This passivity is typically characterized by a refusal to step into what God has called a man to do.

What we see in Solomon's story is an impressive rejection of passivity. He relentlessly engaged his bride's heart. Remember, he leaped like a stag over the mountains. He kept pursuing. He tried to woo her out of the cleft of the rock. This was not a passive man. Therefore, his strength and leadership were celebrated on his wedding day. He stewarded his power well.

Men, let me plead with you: The greatest fight of your life is not lust. You may think it is, but it isn't. The greatest fight of your life will be rejecting the passivity that has infected your heart since the fall. Your natural default, especially as it pertains to sacrificial leadership of your wife, will be to mutely witness.

Some may say, "You know, Matt, I've met a lot of men who aren't passive at all. They're actually way too aggressive."

And I would say that those men are overcompensating for their passivity.

That kind of aggressive, obnoxious behavior is a faux masculinity that takes the easy path of reaction and impulse rather than the harder path of peace and patience and servanthood.

I've seen both extremes time and again, especially in marital counseling. So many men just won't lead. They won't step into the fray. They won't engage. They won't own what God has given them to own.

They say it's too hard.

They don't mind difficulty at work or in sports or fitness or figuring out how to fix something, but when it comes to the difficulty of a relationship, suddenly they wimp out. This challenge out of all the challenges is the one that matters most!

Look, being a man according to God's Word is hard. Being a boy who shaves is pretty easy. But being a real man requires self-sacrifice. Your life is laid down for the good of your wife, for the good of your children.

This kind of commitment seems evident in Solomon's wedding. His intentionality showed. His commitment was public. His desire and ability to lead with strength and dignity and honor were clearly confirmed.

This kind of strength comes from the Lord. Men, in the greatest fight of your life, the daily dying to yourself in the rejection of passivity and the acceptance of responsibility, you will need to rely totally on the grace of God in Christ. But this is a good place to secure your trust because the Bible says that God's grace is power.

We can see the marks of God's power all over Solomon's wedding day. The whole thing was colored by the grace of God. And when your relationship is patterned that way, you will see similar celebrations in your own wedding ceremony and subsequently in your married life.

CHAPTER FIVE

"AND THE TWO BECOME ONE FLESH"

We followed our newly wedded couple through their romantic Song from their first meeting through dating, courtship, and right up to their wedding ceremony. Next, leaving no aspect of their relationship to our imagination, they ask us to follow them to the honeymoon suite.

There's no getting around it. This is exactly what was happening in Song of Solomon 4. They sang about sex on their wedding night. When you adequately interpret the poetry, the actions described are fairly graphic. But it's not crude. It's not inappropriate.

What we see is the outpouring and unleashing of desires that were held in check by God's grace working through the couple's godly will to obey. Solomon and his bride restrained themselves throughout their relationship while growing closer emotionally and spiritually. They became very intimate in their relationship, but even as sexual desire for each other grew, they didn't stir that love before its time.

But now it's time. They made their vows before the witness of their community and families. They pledged before God and each other to *ahava* love, no matter what—all the way until death. The covenant was sealed, and now they get to make the proverbial drive from the reception to the hotel.

When you marry your spouse, if your wedding day is the culmination of a long period of physical restraint, you will probably experience a similar feeling. Maybe you'll hop on a plane to your honeymoon spot, land, rent a car, and make the drive to your honeymoon suite. You'll be nervous and excited and a little scared, but a lot excited and sort of anxious and a very whole lot excited. You know that what you've held back for all this time is now sanctioned.

There's another thing that may happen on the honeymoon night—something that probably happens more often than people care to admit: when a married couple finally meet each other sexually for the first time, when it's over, they may think, *That's it?* Between the buildup of anticipation, the nirvana-like category our culture has assigned sex, and the long, long wait, sometimes that first time is built up out of proportion. More weight is given to it than ought to be. We need to have some caution when reading about Solomon and his bride's first time. If we misread it, we may set ourselves up for having our joy stolen.

Similarly, if you've been married a long while, if you've got kids, you work long hours, and you and your spouse have been racking up the years in age, you may read Song of Solomon 4 and think, *What fairy tale did this come out of? This is ridiculous.*

Thus, we need another caution. Remember that this chapter covers what we may call "ideal sex"—honeymoon sex between a couple who have actively kept themselves chaste while connecting deeply with each other on every other level. The sex depicted in Song of Solomon 4 is like the throwing open of a dam to release all the wonderful pressure of the nonsexual intimacy building up in their relationship. Their hearts were full and hopeful. What's depicted is ideal sex. However, I think we can still pull some principles out of this text for our own sex lives well into marriage, even if you can barely remember your honeymoon night or even if you'd prefer to forget it. This fourth chapter of Solomon's Song shows us, from God's perspective, what sex is meant to be. And it starts by not being in a hurry to start.

SEX IS ROMANTIC

When you're making love to a soul and not a physical body, there's this unbelievably powerful, fulfilling, beautiful thing that occurs. Song of Solomon 4:1 begins with a declaration that I find unbelievably profound: "Behold, you are beautiful, my love, behold, you are beautiful! Your eyes are doves behind your veil. Your hair is like a flock of goats leaping down the slopes of Gilead."

What was he talking about? Well, he was talking about her eyes, but he *wasn't* talking about her eyes. He was commenting on her appearance, but he *wasn't* just saying, "You're hot," or whatever. That can be a nice thing to say at the right time, if your woman appreciates that, but "You're hot" doesn't really get the depth of his feeling here. In giving his appraisal of her appearance, Solomon was really romantically *approving* of her. More than that, he was delighting in her.

So there they were in the honeymoon suite. He had his tux on. She was wearing her dress. He looked at her. They were all alone. The sixty groomsmen and sixty bridesmaids were left behind. And finally together, alone, on the precipice of long-forbidden intimacy, he looked deep into her eyes—into her soul, really—and said, "You are beautiful."

"Behold!" he said. "You are beautiful!" He was captivated by her, body and soul. He didn't say, "I like your eyes." He dug deep. He kept pulling out the poetry. He didn't turn off the poetry when they finally got married, as if the work was done, as if all his romantic effort was simply in getting a woman to say yes so he could put the relationship on autopilot. He said, "Your eyes are doves ... Your hair is like a flock of goats leaping down the slopes of Gilead."

Now, in case you don't know better, men, you're probably going to need to update your language a bit. Don't try saying this exact stuff to your wife. Don't put the book down, take your wife in your arms, and say, "Man, your hair reminds me of goats." Probably doesn't translate too well today and will probably end differently for you than for Solomon. So don't steal his words, but do steal his idea.

Solomon continued to survey her beauty and respond with poetic approval:

> Your lips are like a scarlet thread,
>> and your mouth is lovely.
> Your cheeks are like halves of a pomegranate
>> behind your veil.
> Your neck is like the tower of David,
>> built in rows of stone;

on it hang a thousand shields,

all of them shields of warriors. (vv. 3–4)

Once again, it's very clear that these two saved themselves for each other, because we've seen the whole romance from the beginning. It's also very clear that the romance didn't stop on the wedding day. It was carried through into the wedding night. They weren't even undressed yet when Solomon remarked on her captivating presence.

This is such an important principle to remember, especially for men. Notice how Solomon proceeded, husbands. He wasn't quick or rough. He hadn't even touched her yet. He spent the first moments where intimacy began to build by saying, essentially, "Your soul is beautiful."

He wasn't in a hurry. He gazed at her beauty and went step-by-step, slowly praising her—eyes, mouth, cheeks, neck. This whole thing is very, very romantic. Notice he hadn't even gone below her neck yet. (Yet!) He didn't say, "Man, your eyes are pretty. And those breasts!" No, he took his time. He started from the top and worked his way slowly down, doling out praise in a very measured fashion.

As he did this, what do you think happened to her nerves, her fear, her insecurity? If he had just hauled off and grabbed her right off the bat, her guard would likely have gone right back up again. But he slowly disarmed her before he disrobed her. We know from the previous chapters that she likely carried around some insecurity about her body, about her appearance, as nearly every woman does. Solomon knew this. And because Solomon was very wise, he also knew that insecure women do not feel safe. Nor do they feel free and sexually uninhibited.

Do you remember that old country song "Older Women (Are Beautiful Lovers)"? No, you're probably not Spotifying it. But that song by Ronnie McDowell is interestingly enough pretty truthful— at least as far as the premise goes that the older a woman gets, usually the more comfortable in her body she becomes. She becomes more comfortable with who she is. The song is sort of a celebration of that idea, I think. Solomon didn't marry an older woman, but he understood the same principle: unless and until his bride felt confident in her own skin—and felt confident that Solomon was confident in her—she wouldn't be ready to give herself fully to him.

And, of course, he was also aware that women don't get turned on the same way men do. Unlike men, most women aren't always sexually "ready to go." They need some time, some tending to. You've probably heard the old adage that women aren't microwaves but Crock-Pots. So Solomon warmed her up. And what we see in his slowness, his poetry, his wise understanding of how she was wired and what she needed to hear is that marital sex according to God's Word is romantic.

SEX IS TENDER

What Solomon did to romance his bride initiated deeper levels of intimacy and vulnerability. As a result, as this chapter progresses, we see increasing openness. He next moved to behold her physical beauty more fully.

"Your two breasts are like two fawns, twins of a gazelle, that graze among the lilies" (4:5). Her dress was at least half off as she stood topless before him, and he praised her still, poetically complimenting her breasts.

This metaphor may be a little difficult to decipher, but let me see if I can break it down for you. Fawns are baby deer, right? Now, if you saw two baby deer grazing among the lilies, how would you approach them? Let's assume you have some sense and an appreciation of nature. What do you do? Well, for instance, you don't tackle fawns. You approach them quietly and gingerly. And if they don't run away as you slowly approach, you don't ring theirs necks when you get there, right?

Are you following me here?

We see in this portion of the text that marital sex is not only romantic but also gentle.

I often hear guys complain about the frequency of sex in their marriage, but I can tell by the things they say and the way they say those things that they may be their own worst problem. I want to say to them, "Maybe if you quit groping your wife, she'd be more interested."

Women respond to slowness and gentleness. Once you've reached the point of intercourse, she may want you to move more quickly and touch more firmly, but most women can't get to that point until they've felt wooed into it. They want to feel safe and secure. They want to feel embraced more than grabbed, caressed more than groped.

Make no mistake: Solomon looked at his wife's naked breasts. He was going to touch them and kiss them. He wanted to go further. But he was going about the whole thing with an evident tenderness. He was interested in more than his own gratification; he wanted his bride to feel sexual pleasure too—but beyond that, he wanted her to feel loved.

This is another reason pornography is so dangerous. It makes men sexually stupid. You might think it's showing you advanced stuff, the right techniques, the apex of sexual activity, but it's so remedial. It's less than remedial, actually, because it is fake. Those performers may actually be having sex, but they are doing just that: performing. They aren't making love. And the whole scene is not an accurate depiction of two people expressing love for each other through sex but rather a facade, a ruse, an illusion of intimacy. The whole thing is designed to gratify the male viewer; it is sex as a lustful man would imagine it.

When young men become trained by pornography, they get married and expect things from their wives that their wives aren't interested in or can't even do. It leads to frustration and anger and shame and insecurity. Pornography doesn't show you what sex is; it shows you what male lust is.

Sex the way God created it to be is very romantic and, yes, very intense, but also very tender. Let's talk about that intensity, though.

SEX IS PASSIONATE

In the Song of Solomon 4:6, our new husband declared from the joy of the honeymoon suite: "Until the day breathes and the shadows flee, I will go away to the mountain of myrrh and the hill of frankincense."

In case you're not tracking, he basically said, "We're going to be here for a while." He wanted to do this until the sun came up! When he talked about the mountain and the hill, he wasn't talking about going for a hike. He was referring to her, or to certain parts of her, and how he intended to tend to them for a long, long time.

It's important to take this into consideration because as we see in the text that marital sex is meant to be romantic and tender, it's not coldly methodical. He showed restraint in this time of foreplay, but he wasn't devoid of passion. He was intoxicated by her. He couldn't get enough of her. The sexual fire burning within him—that God put there for his wife—was growing hotter and hotter. Not only does God want married sex to be romantic and tender, but he also wants it to be passionate.

The sex described between our newlyweds was exhilarating. I mean, I don't really know if Solomon had the stamina to do what he said he was going to do, but he sure meant to try. Fundamentally what he said is richer than what he planned to do with her. He was basically saying, "I'm not going anywhere. I'm here. I've got nowhere else I want to be." Whether they were moving slowly or more quickly, he wasn't setting her up for a "wham, bam, thank you, ma'am." He wasn't checking his watch, looking over her shoulder at the television, thinking about work, or stressing about the yard. He was totally in the moment, and he declared that *he didn't want the moment to end*.

This is what we should desire for the marriage bed. Not in a hurry, not in a rush. Not thinking about a thousand different things. No distractions, no interruptions. Ideally, the sex is so loving that it builds itself up, fuels itself, and keeps stoking the passion as it proceeds.

Consider chapter 4, verse 7: "You are altogether beautiful, my love; there is no flaw in you."

He hasn't let up, has he? When he said "You are altogether beautiful," we are meant to assume that he saw her in her entirety. She was completely naked. Culturally, this was a time when a woman's figure was entirely hidden by her dress. They didn't wear formfitting clothes. So this was likely the first time Solomon was able to consider the size of her breasts, the roundness of her hips, or the shape of her legs.

She must have been nervous about this too! What if he saw something he didn't like? Would he have been able to disguise some disappointment? She was probably thinking, *I hope he likes this. I hope he will approve of me. I hope I don't disappoint him.*

Solomon didn't miss a beat. "You're flawless," he said. He saw his bride standing naked before him, and in a moment every married couple must experience, he had the opportunity to bring either grace or judgment. Like that very first couple in history, they were exposed to each other. Before sin entered the world, Adam and Eve were "naked and unashamed." This is the spirit of sexuality, intimacy, and security every married couple ought to strive for, with the husband taking responsibility to lead the way.

Solomon and his bride were in their honeymoon chamber, naked and unashamed.

Our groom sought to put his wife at ease because of his love for her. And he was *in love with her*. He was crazy about her. Nothing could change that.

> Come with me from Lebanon, my bride;
>> come with me from Lebanon.
> Depart from the peak of Amana,
>> from the peak of Senir and Hermon,
> from the dens of lions,
>> from the mountains of leopards. (v. 8)

What in the world was going on? Did they get bored and go to the zoo?

No, he was out of his mind with passion for her. There were mountain peaks, wild animals—a romantic ferocity, a *passion* taking place. They were being transported! Maybe you've heard some sexual encounters described as out-of-body experiences. This was one of those. They felt swept away. The passion was so great that this sex became about more than sex and physical gratification. It became the culmination and the means of something greater, something beyond themselves.

Solomon cried out to her, "Come with me," and he thereby demonstrated his gracious leading of her into passionate pleasure. "Take hold of my love," he was saying. "I want to sweep you away and take you to dazzling heights of love." One commentator remarked, "This seems to be simply the bridegroom rejoicing over the bride, the meaning being, 'Give thyself up to me'—thou art mine; look away from the past, and delight thyself in the future."[1]

The passion in their sex was not simply about sexual appetite and urges. It was indicative of the goal of marriage, that a man and woman would become "one flesh" (Gen. 2:24). A real union was taking place. They were becoming something different.

When a husband and wife really connect sexually, the passion can be overwhelming. If you are married, perhaps you know this experience quite well. It may not happen the same way every time, but when you're both totally in sync, firing on all cylinders, and the sexual encounter is taking place after an obvious connection that is emotional and spiritual, it is entirely different from simply "having sex." And Solomon's poetic tongue can't and won't stop:

You have captivated my heart, my sister, my bride;
> you have captivated my heart with one glance
>> of your eyes,
> with one jewel of your necklace.
How beautiful is your love, my sister, my bride!
> How much better is your love than wine,
> and the fragrance of your oils than any spice!
Your lips drip nectar, my bride;
> honey and milk are under your tongue;
> the fragrance of your garments is like the
>> fragrance of Lebanon (vv. 9–11).

He kissed her passionately, sensuously. He found her *delicious*. In an odd way, you could almost say that his passionate loving of her was gluttonous. To describe her taste like nectar and honey and milk was a way to say he was feasting on her passion. And in fact, in Song of Solomon 5:1, the lovers were told to "be drunk with love!" Much like the young husband is told in Proverbs 5:19 to "be intoxicated always" by his wife's love.

Obviously, there are ways that lust and unrestrained appetites can masquerade as passion. We need to make an effort not to confuse passion with quickness or forcefulness. Everything from porn to romance novels seems to get this wrong, almost always conflating passion with roughness. A married couple may progress into a degree of vigorousness in sex that they mutually agree is appropriate, of course, but the romance and the tenderness must remain. And the passion we see here, as exhilarating and "drunk" as it was, was not how the sex began. Nor was it the pace of one party against the restraint of the other. Instead, this passion was the result of husband and wife so connected on every level, and so worked up from all the seduction and wooing before intercourse, that they were jointly stirred, aroused, and impassioned.

There is no limit on this kind of passion. Betsy Ricucci wrote, "Within the context of covenant love and mutual service, no amount of passion is excessive. Scripture says our sexual intimacy should be exhilarating."[2]

To trade in this kind of passion, as free and fun and fiery as it can be, for the basic giving in to libidinous urges is to debase sex, which even married couples can do. Just because a married couple agrees on some sexual behavior does not sanctify that behavior. There is a way for even Christian married couples to have sex "in the passion of lust like the Gentiles who do not know God" (1 Thess. 4:5).

The couple in the Song of Solomon possessed a passion akin to adoration. It was awash with glory, not about urges but unction.

The union of husband and wife comes to fruition through sexual intimacy, and it makes their sex about more than sex. And this is why, biblically speaking, sex has a sacredness to it.

SEX IS HOLY

The passion continues as we proceed through the fourth chapter, but the tone changes a bit. It seems evident that their passionate experience revealed to them something special about marital sex, something sex outside of marriage can never be. Solomon said:

> A garden locked is my sister, my bride,
>   a spring locked, a fountain sealed.

Your shoots are an orchard of pomegranates
>with all choicest fruits,
>henna with nard,
nard and saffron, calamus and cinnamon,
>with all trees of frankincense,
myrrh and aloes,
>with all choice spices—
a garden fountain, a well of living water,
>and flowing streams from Lebanon. (vv. 12–15)

What we know about Solomon from the book of Ecclesiastes is that he was quite the botanist. He built not only gardens but also full-on national forests. The guy's green thumb was unreal. He spent a very large portion of his life building gardens in Jerusalem. In fact, if we were to hop on a plane right now and fly to the west or east side of Jerusalem, we would see these massive craters that are called the Pools of Solomon. He built them to water the forests he had planted. This guy knew his stuff.

What he did here in this passage, then, was list the rarest, most expensive, and most sought-after plants, flowers, and spices. And he's comparing those things to his bride. He said, "Your body is like an impossible garden, the dream garden, the stuff of mythology!" Because you can't grow cinnamon in the same place that you grow pomegranates, for instance. But as he passionately drank in her body, as their souls became mingled together in the purest of marital sex, he proclaimed, "Your body is the most perfect place, and it's being discovered for the first time."

Think of the fabled lost city of Atlantis or El Dorado. Places of legend, places that, if they even exist, have been hidden for centuries.

He compared her to the discovery of a lost garden that existed only in his imagination; it was locked up and hidden for years. Until he discovered it.

But this was bigger than just a myth found to be true. It was a parallel discovery to the wonder of God's glory. The freedom of the marriage bed is seen here to be a correlation of, for instance, entering the Holy of Holies after being forbidden access for so long.

I don't want to overstate it. This is an analogy, not an equation. But it's a good, biblical analogy. There was something *holy* taking place between husband and wife. It was sacred, special, unique.

"Holy" has often been defined as "being set apart for special use." Sex certainly fits that description. It is not for everybody. It is set aside for special use in marriage. Sex is holy.

At that moment, Solomon was in a way saying, "You know, I could have sexual intercourse with any woman, but what's happening here is well beyond our physical bodies and just sex." There was a friendship that had been built. There was real, sacrificial love. There was genuine care for the soul.

Physically speaking, they had a great time, of course, but there was something behind his desire to touch her that was greater than testosterone or the desire for an orgasm. As C. S. Lewis wrote, "Pleasures are shafts of the glory as it strikes our sensibility.... Make every pleasure into a channel of adoration."[3] He was speaking of the Christian's need to follow every earthly pleasure back to its source in the God who is the giver of every good thing (see James 1:17), that he might get the glory.

And that is why sex is holy—it is meant to remind us of the God who gave it to us, who takes joy in union with his people. We don't need to overspiritualize sex to see it this way; we just need to approach it the way the Bible ordained and be grateful for it. Seeing sex as holy will also help us love our spouses more greatly. Gary Thomas wrote:

> Sex is about physical touch, to be sure, but it is about far more than physical touch. It is about what is going on inside us. Developing a fulfilling sex life means I concern myself more with bringing generosity and service to bed than with bringing washboard abdomens. It means I see my wife as a holy temple of God, not just as a tantalizing human body. It even means that sex becomes a form of physical prayer—a picture of heavenly intimacy that rivals the *shekinah* glory of old.[4]

SEX IS RECIPROCAL

So far in the fourth chapter of Solomon's Song, we've heard only from Solomon. It's good that he took the lead in the honeymoon suite, setting the tone for his bride so she knew he would be romantic and tender and passionate, while also maintaining the boundaries God set up for marital sex. He made her feel safe and secure, and because of that, she felt unashamed and free and uninhibited.

She responded, "Awake, O north wind, and come, O south wind! Blow upon my garden, let its spices flow" (v. 16).

This is probably pretty much what you think it is.

Solomon brought her to the point of rapture. She was totally surrendered. He told her she was beautiful with her dress on, which was important. He told her she was beautiful with her dress off, which was also important. He kissed every part of her body, taking his time, tending to her in the right places at the right pace, and in Song of Solomon 4:16 she essentially called out to him to "bring it."

The north wind in Jewish symbolism represents strength. He said he planned to tend to her mountains and hills until daybreak, and she replied, "I'll bring the Gatorade." (Not really, but kinda.) "Awake, O north wind" means, basically, "I hope you're not almost done!"

But the south wind is a little different. The south wind, as the reciprocal of the north wind, represents gentleness. "Take me!" she cried out. "But continue to be gently passionate." She wanted it to last because she was enjoying it too; drunk on passion right alongside him; enraptured, aroused, and reciprocating his love.

What we see here in an ideal sexual encounter between husband and wife is a mutually enjoyable and mutually expressive love. And it can remind us that men desire for their wives to desire them too.

I think sometimes what happens when there are intimacy issues in marriages, particularly when women have intimacy issues, is that they know their husbands' desires for sex, but somehow they've come to see sex as dirty or forbidden. Or maybe they've come to think that it is sinful for a woman to enjoy sex or that it makes her unholy or unfeminine or immodest. So many wives will have sex with their husbands, but they avoid passionate intimacy. Sometimes there's a block there.

Many men are trying to do the right thing, and they're trying to care for their wives and figure out what it is that will please them sexually, but the intimacy isn't working. The husband will slow down, but his wife freezes up. He'll speed up, but that makes things worse.

This is one of those areas in our lives where if we're not careful, the little foxes will absolutely destroy the garden. If you're in this situation right now, consider seeking help from a trusted Christian counselor. Maybe you need to seek out a recovery program for sexual abuse, pornography, or other kinds of trauma. This could be especially helpful if you're able to look back and pinpoint where wounds have prevented intimacy. This is not an easy thing to approach, and it's not a light thing to process. It is complex and heavy, and while I can't cover the fullness of its complexity in the space of this book, I don't want you to assume that's because I don't think it's a big deal. If there is a real barrier here in your marriage, if intimacy (sexual or otherwise) is being blocked because of wounds, insecurities, or traumas from your past, for your own spiritual and emotional health and for the health of your marriage, please seek help.

Women, assuming you are able, I have to tell you that your husband is not seeking just sexual willingness from you but sexual eagerness. They are not the same thing. Many women think that all their husbands want is sexual release. Of course men want sexual release, but you might be surprised to know that most men cannot find even that release fulfilling if they know their wives did not enjoy the experience.

In her book *For Women Only*, Shaunti Feldhahn revealed the results of a professional survey of men that asked this question:

> With regard to sex, for some men it is sufficient to be sexually gratified whenever they want. For other men it is also important to feel wanted and desired by their wife. How important is it to you to also feel sexually wanted and desired by your wife?[5]

Feldhahn wrote:

> This topic earned the highest degree of unanimity
> of any question: 97 percent of men said "getting
> enough sex" wasn't, by itself, enough—they wanted
> to feel wanted.
>
> One man I interviewed summed it up like this:
> "Everyone thinks women are more emotional than
> men. And everyone thinks that when it comes to
> sex, guys just want to 'do it,' and women are more
> into the emotion and cuddling of it. So women
> think there are no emotions there. But there *are*,
> and when you say no, you are messing with all
> those emotions."
>
> And it's not only a flat "no" that hurts. The sur-
> vey showed that *even if they were getting all the sex they
> wanted*, three out of four men would still feel empty
> if their wife wasn't both engaged and satisfied.[6]

The truth is, for men, sexual reciprocity is extraordinarily pleasing and satisfying in ways mere sexual release is not.

Whether Solomon's bride knew this or not, she was eager to
please—*and to be pleased*. "That mythic garden you were just singing about?" she basically said at the end of verse 16. "Come eat its
choicest fruits." She called her groom to come indulge in her and
enjoy her.

And when sex is reciprocal and mutually enjoyable, it becomes
as mutually fulfilling as it can be.

SEX IS FULFILLING

Are Solomon and his bride blowing you away yet? This dude was masterful with the poetry, and she ate it all up. He led expertly, and she responded joyfully. But I wonder if we shouldn't get the wrong idea. This was their first night together, their first attempt at this sex thing, and I'm willing to bet neither of them was as good at it that night as they would be after many years together. I'd bet neither one of them had very good sexual technique.

I'm sure those of you who are not virgins can recall your first time. I don't know how you'd grade yourself, but even if it was your wedding night and therefore was superspecial, more than likely, if you're honest, you were thinking, *That's it?*

Solomon and his bride moved wonderfully toward satisfaction, but there's indication that they weren't experts at this stuff right away. They were completely inexperienced. They hadn't learned each other's bodies yet, so we're not going to call them experts as far as technique goes. And yet, they thoroughly enjoyed sex.

Once again, we see that sex is not about technique but rather finding ourselves in the rhythm of how God designed sex to be. And as we turn the corner now into Song of Solomon chapter 5, we see the voice of God reflected in the chiming in of others, perhaps still ringing in their ears from the celebration of their wedding: "Eat, friends, drink, and be drunk with love!" (v. 1).

Solomon and his bride consummated their marriage at this point. They were lying in the bed (it had apparently been about a day and a half!), and the outside voice passing judgment on their wedding night experience was well pleased. Their entire experience was *very pleasing* to God. "Good job," he said. "Well done. Keep it up."

How pleasing was it to God? I mean, they were lounging in bed, trying to recover, sighing, "Oh, we're so full," and God said, "Have some more."

God wants married couples to know that sex is his gift to them. And God does not give gifts to people so they *won't* enjoy them. If he gives you steak, he wants you to savor it. If he gives you wine, he wants you to enjoy it. And when he gives a couple sex in the covenant of marriage, he wants them to indulge in it. The NIV translates the end of Song of Solomon 5:1 this way: "Drink your fill of love." Why would he tell us to drink up if he didn't want us to be fully satisfied?

If you put Song of Solomon 4 next to any romantic comedy or any porn site on the web, I don't know any sane man or woman who'd say, "Yeah, I'll take the movie. I'll take the porn." If you want to see sex as God created it to be, Song of Solomon 4 is it. When you bring in the context of what led to this moment in the Song as well as the Bible's teaching on sex in other books, you can see that God is not stingy with joy when it comes to sexuality. If he gives you a gift, he wants you to enjoy it as it is designed to be enjoyed, which will ultimately lead to your satisfaction—not only with the gift itself but also with himself as the Giver.

Sex in the Song of Solomon is romantic, gentle, passionate, holy, and reciprocal. Because of all that, it is deeply satisfying for both the married couple and for God. When we steward sexuality in the appropriate biblical way, it can remind us to enjoy sex without making it an idol, to engage in it in a way that serves our greater good, which is ultimately trusting in the grace of God in Christ.

SEX IS ABOUT THE GOSPEL

Maybe you've read through Song of Solomon 4 and thought, *You know, this sounds like a really beautiful thing, but I'm a messed-up person and this is a broken world, and it all seems pretty unrealistic.*

All of us have been wounded and hurt in some way. We're all insecure, fearful, and broken. Maybe you are a husband thinking, *I've already blown it. I haven't led my wife like Solomon, so that ship has sailed.* Maybe you're a wife thinking, *I don't want to be unresponsive to my husband, but I don't know how to make myself enjoy this.*

Human beings are so complex. When you factor in sin, trauma, insecurity, and anxiety, our brokenness becomes part of that complexity. We can begin to feel indecipherable, unfixable.

When I was growing up, one thing I couldn't figure out was what was going on at church. Going to church always confused me. Everybody seemed so happy, and I couldn't figure out why. If you're relatively new to church, have you ever tried to figure out why the people there raise their hands? 'Cause that's goofy, isn't it? Are they trying to ask questions of the guy up front?

Or if you just don't understand this whole Christianity thing, you may get really confused about why people become emotional when it comes to the thought of God. What's going on inside of them that thinking about some God up in heaven would make them weep?

So I want to clue you in because it's something that I learned over time by God's grace working in my life through the Christian message. What people are celebrating is that while we were at our worst, Jesus still loved us.

What made me love Christ wasn't that all of a sudden I figured out how to do life. What made me love Christ is that when I was at my worst, when I was at my lowest point, when I absolutely could not clean myself up and there was nothing anybody could do with me, right at that moment, Christ said, "I'll take that one. That's the one I want."

You know the Bible calls the church Christ's bride. So it's like standing before Jesus, completely exposed, all of our flaws and insecurities and—worse than that—our sins are right there in front of his face, and against all reason and rationale, the song of grace becomes startlingly, exhilaratingly true because the Groom looks at us and declares us beautiful. Spotless. Righteous. Justified.

This is the gospel. It is important to admit, believers in Jesus, that Christians are not more moral than anyone else. The essence of the gospel and what we celebrate is not that "we can" but that *Christ did.*

Intimacy is hard for broken people. We need Jesus. We need his help. But when you've gotten closer and closer to the incredible reality that God chose you, forgave you, and approved of you despite your sin, all because of Jesus Christ, that grace is satisfying and empowering, and it can be carried over into your marriage. It can be carried over in the way you respond to your spouse, confident and free because of Christ's work in your life. It can be carried over in the way you forgive your spouse's sins and overlook his or her imperfections, as a way of sharing what God has given you.

In this way, sex can be about the gospel, if we're mindful enough to make it so. If Jesus wanted the broken version of you, can you find the strength to want your broken spouse? In Christ, it is possible—it just has to be worked and fought for.

Love the gift of sex and love your spouse, but it's not technique or romance that makes sex like they had in Song of Solomon 4 possible—it's Jesus. He—and he alone—reconciled what went so wrong in Genesis 3.

Can you have pleasurable sex outside of life in Jesus? Sure. But it can't be all that he designed it to be. In the end, it won't draw you any closer to the person you're having sex with. It certainly won't draw you closer to God, who alone satisfies completely. But married sex *can* draw you closer to God and your spouse, and one of the ways it does that is by pointing away from sex and toward the gospel of Jesus Christ.

Sex is good, but it's not built for eternity. It won't be around forever. Neither will marriage, for that matter. No, marriage and sex are good, but Jesus is better. He is better than everything in life. He is better than life itself. He *is* life!

CHAPTER SIX

FIGHTING FAIR

Before I proposed to Lauren and while we were still in the courtship stage, we confronted certain issues over and over again. Eventually it became a cause for concern. I fully admit there were lots of things at that time I did not handle well, and in fact, even today I feel pangs of regret (and have to preach the gospel to myself!). But at the time, I was moved enough by the recurring issues to go speak to one of my mentors, David.

I asked him about these consistent fights that kept coming up, and I told him I didn't know what to do. I asked him, "Should I marry a woman whom I still get in fights with? Shouldn't we be beyond this? We're not even married yet, and already we're fighting."

I'll never forget what David said to me. "Brother, you are going to fight with someone for the rest of your life. Do you want it to be Lauren?"

He was telling me that when you get married, conflict isn't going anywhere. I mean, I sort of knew that, but I guess I thought it should be easier if you've found the right woman. That's exactly where David pressed. "Matt, is Lauren the one you want to fight with for the rest of your life? Whoever you marry, you're going to fight with. If it's not Lauren, it will be somebody else."

I could have taken his counsel as somewhat discouraging, to be sure. But I found it both encouraging and refreshing. The truth is that none of us have "arrived." And this side of heaven, none of us ever will. We all are being sanctified, and we will always be in the process of sanctification until the Lord returns and we are caught up into glory. Until then, we may have areas of victory in our lives, places we make improvements and learn to be better at repenting, but the flesh will always be there. We will always be somewhat broken, and we will never be perfect.

We need to remember every day that we are sinners, and to be a sinner means to be essentially self-centered, and to be essentially self-centered means we are destined for conflict in our relationships.

Since the Spirit's process of sanctification is progressive, we will never be where we should be, but God in his grace will use the circumstances and the relationships in our lives to sharpen us, shape us, and make us more and more who he wants us to be.

One of my favorite books on marriage is by Gary Thomas. The title is *Sacred Marriage*, and the tagline for the book is this: "What if God designed marriage to make us holy more than to make us happy?" I literally bought the book because of that tagline. It is so gutsy. Some people might look at that subtitle and think, *So it's supposed to make me holy but miserable?* Those people probably aren't thinking, *All right, let's give it a shot*. An author would probably sell more marriage books if he promised absolute happiness to readers.

But I bought the book because I loved the honesty and authenticity of it. It's a great book because it does not shy away from the real purpose of marriage, which is to glorify God, and it's completely truthful about the way God designed marriage to give him glory. An integral part of marriage's design is the sanctifying work that takes place between two sinners in close proximity, learning to love each other.

The bottom line is this: conflict is going to be a part of your relationship. It's going to be a part of even the healthiest, most romantic, most passionate relationships. In fact, I have found that the more passion you possess in *loving* oftentimes translates to more passion in fighting. Passionate personality types tend to do both pretty well.

One of my best friends has an extremely passionate personality, very gregarious, very excitable. And he married a woman who is very similar in that regard. I remember when they started dating, I was thinking, *Oh my gosh. What happens if they have children?* And sure enough, true to form, after over a decade of marriage, and several kids later, they still love really well and they still fight pretty often.

Maybe you'll find it oddly comforting to know that conflict is a natural part of being married. It doesn't mean conflict is always great. It doesn't mean that a conflict-filled marriage is a good thing that doesn't need a lot of work. Just because two Christians love Jesus and love each other doesn't mean all of life is going to be smooth sailing.

Even redeemed sinners who love each other obey God's Word imperfectly. This is one of the things that makes God's grace so amazing—his long-suffering patience with us. In this chapter I hope to share some thoughts from the Song of Solomon that may help you reflect God's long-suffering patience with your spouse.

To begin, we ought to consider the root of our conflicts.

UNMET EXPECTATIONS

Twenty percent of Solomon's Song covers conflict. That's a pretty significant percentage, don't you think? As I said before, I think the only people who don't realize that marriage is going to be difficult are engaged people. They're in a blissful state where it's hard to think straight about the future. What we see in Song of Solomon 5 helps give us clarity about the marriage relationship and sobers us up a little.

We've just glimpsed the joy of their honeymoon night, and it's not too long after that their first conflict occurred. "I slept, but my heart was awake. A sound! My beloved is knocking. 'Open to me, my sister, my love, my dove, my perfect one, for my head is wet with dew, my locks with the drops of the night'" (v. 2).

Solomon had been working all day long. We gather this from the reference to his head being "wet with dew." He'd been working out in the fields, and he was tired and sweaty and ready to come home.

It seems that he came home pretty late, late enough that his wife had already showered and gone to bed: "I had put off my garment; how could I put it on? I had bathed my feet; how could I soil them?" (v. 3).

To set the scene properly, Solomon was coming home after a very long day, and on his way home he probably started thinking about what being home would be like. He thought about his wife and how nice it would be to be with her. She would welcome him, give him a big kiss, have food waiting for him. He was probably even thinking about petting those fawns, right?

But she already bathed, put on her nightie, went to bed, and fell asleep. She officially took the "not tonight" position.

It's a very typical scene in married life, one that is rehearsed in countless households over many, many days. The essential elements of this moment play out in a million different ways throughout the life of a relationship. It doesn't have to be about a husband coming home tired and late from work, expecting his wife to have a satisfying welcome waiting. It's about any time we build up in our minds how our partners should please us or care for us and he or she fails to deliver as we wanted.

Really, all frustration is birthed out of unmet expectations, and so is nearly every conflict.

Look closely at Solomon's response to his expectations not being met. There's one thing he did that I think is a correct response to unmet expectations, and there's another thing he did that I think, especially in the midst of conflict, isn't always a correct response but is sometimes necessary. He came to the door with expectation about what was going to happen, and she shut him down. Here's his initial response as told by his wife:

> My beloved put his hand to the latch,
> and my heart was thrilled within me.
> I arose to open to my beloved,
> and my hands dripped with myrrh,
> my fingers with liquid myrrh,
> on the handles of the bolt.

I opened to my beloved,
> but my beloved had turned and gone.
My soul failed me when he spoke.
I sought him, but found him not;
> I called him, but he gave no answer. (vv. 4–6)

She shut down the sexual rendezvous, and he didn't get angry. He didn't react. He didn't blow up. When he reached out to touch the latch, he communicated something significant, because that action was sort of like a valentine in their culture: a sign that said, "Well, I know you're turning me down, but I love you anyway."

His expectations were unmet, and he was frustrated, but he took a moment to say, "I love you."

As so often happens in our relationships, sometimes we can say the right things, but our hearts are not in the right place. We should trust that Solomon meant this statement, that when he touched the latch for her to hear, he was not feigning love. But it doesn't mean he wasn't frustrated. So what did he do next?

He left. He didn't wash and then get in bed with her. He went for a walk.

Apparently, Solomon wanted to walk off some of his frustration. (We'll see a little bit of how he dealt with it in the next few verses.)

His wife realized he left, so she bolted out of bed to look for him.

Does any of this sound familiar? Your conflicts in marriage may not play out in exactly this same way, but aren't they similar? Have you ever been in a fight, ever experienced a frustration so difficult that one of you felt led to leave the marriage bed? Maybe one of you went to sleep on the couch or in the guest room, or maybe you

FIGHTING FAIR / **149**

jumped in the car to go for a drive. Then the other spouse got up and went looking.

It's a very tender moment. Even in tension there can be tenderness. Even in conflict there can be reminders of love. And the important thing to remember in these moments—in quiet conflict or all-out verbal arguments—is how God would have us fight with each other. He knows the fights are going to happen because we're sinners. But we can learn to fight fair, and we can learn a few things from Solomon and his wife about how to do that. When expectations are not met, by God's grace we can take control of our minds and put into practice some healthy ways of dealing with our conflict. Here's one of the first healthy practices:

RESPOND; DON'T REACT

One of the rules right out of the gate is that we have to be careful not to *react* to things that upset us. Reaction shows a serious lack of self-control and maturity. Notice that Solomon didn't just blow up at his wife and go on about how she didn't love him or respect him or care about him. None of that happened. Instead, he basically said, "Okay, I get it. I love you." His heart may still have been full of frustration, but he controlled himself and responded to his wife, rather than reacting to her. Then he took his frustration elsewhere.

I'm not saying this was necessarily the right thing to do, but we'll discuss that shortly. In the meantime, let's learn something valuable from Solomon's example. In conflict, we must be very careful not to get caught up in reacting to the things that bother us. That can quickly get out of control, and suddenly the argument takes on a momentum of its own. In those moments, we become slaves to our emotions and impulses. That's not a healthy way to talk to anyone, let alone the person with whom we are supposed to be one flesh.

When expectations are unmet, pride often kicks in. We begin to rehearse in our minds and hearts what we deserve, what we are owed, what the other person ought to do for us. The problem with pride is that it will often make you see things that aren't even there. It has a way of justifying itself and all its demands. Jesus's mother, Mary, referred to this self-delusion when she said that God "has scattered the proud in the thoughts of their hearts" (Luke 1:51).

Pride distorts reality. When we're disappointed about unmet expectations, pride pops up like a little internal defense lawyer giving us all the reasons why our spouses deserve judgment and why we are vindicated in our own righteousness.

But if we were being more thoughtful, we might actually begin to advocate in our imaginations for the person who has frustrated us. In Solomon's situation, perhaps he could have reasoned that his poor wife had been working all day long in the house by herself. As the day grew later and later and it became the wee hours of the night, she probably just became too tired to wait up for him anymore and got in the bed, exhausted.

Then Solomon came, putting on the moves. She wasn't baiting him or insulting him. She just communicated, "Baby, I'm tired. That's not code for 'I hate you.' I'm just worn out."

When pride kicks in, the imaginative reactions of a husband may consist of things such as the following:

"Doesn't she know how hard I've worked?"
"Is it too much to ask for her to have a little fun
when I come home?"
"She must not be attracted to me."

The more frustrated we are, the more we can allow anger to shape our reactions. One telltale sign you've entered that stage of conflict is if you begin listing all your strengths and all your spouse's weaknesses. (By the way, rehearsing all your spouse's failures like this puts you in company with Satan, the great accuser.)

When pride rears up in our hearts, we move so effortlessly into reaction mode. We need to learn how to respond without reacting. There is a difference.

Solomon responded with an "I love you," and then he took a time-out. His wife responded not with fuming and fussing but by trailing after him. Despite the fact that they didn't avoid conflict, they handled it reasonably well—not perfectly, but well. Let's see now how things progressed.

> The watchmen found me
> as they went about in the city;
> they beat me, they bruised me,
> they took away my veil,
> those watchmen of the walls. (5:7)

A physical beating was not actually delivered to the queen by the watchmen. In any era, it's never a good idea to beat up the queen, right? She was using poetic imagery.

Basically, she communicated that she'd been running around, looking for the king everywhere, and everyone she asked about him had no idea where he was. So every time they said, "We haven't seen him. Isn't he with you?" it bruised her soul. She felt emotionally beat up. She was torn up about hurting his feelings. She was worried because he left. She wore herself out with fatigue and anxiety searching for him.

She pleaded with the people she ran into: "I adjure you, O daughters of Jerusalem, if you find my beloved, that you tell him I am sick with love" (v. 8).

This was an important stage in their conflict. Something was broken up. The standoff gave way to healthier responses. Something happened to our queen's heart that I think is rather profound. She went from being unresponsive and cold toward the advances of her husband to running through the castle looking for him, professing that she was sick with love. "I need to find him. I need to grab him. *I need him.*"

When we learn to respond to each other rather than react, we will move much more quickly in our conflict toward resolution and reconciliation. Reactions only stoke the fires of conflict; responses, particularly godly ones, help us snuff out the conflict.

GOING TO GOD

Next, we find out what Solomon was doing. He said, "I love you," in his understated way, then took a walk. Who knows where he went? Maybe he went to the kitchen; maybe he watched *SportsCenter* in the west wing of the castle. We don't really know yet. One thing we do know is that he didn't change his wife's heart. Her heart was changed by God.

Now let me tell you why this truth is important: way too many men and even more women want to use commonsense arguments or manipulation to change the way their spouses feel about or respond toward them. This is absolutely devastating in the end. In our conflicts, we start throwing jabs and we wound each other deeply, *or* we play some kind of manipulation game in order to get our spouses to do what we want.

Some marriage books are predicated on that latter approach. While they are meant to be helpful, they are full of what they might call "best practices"—general rules that work only if both spouses are healthy emotionally and spiritually. But if they're not, the best practices can't work.

What I often see in marriages is that men and women become frustrated because they read these books and learn ways to manipulate their spouse in order to make their spouse indebted to them. So a husband will read one and come away thinking, *Okay, if I do the dishes and vacuum the floor, she'll be responsive to me.* I've even been at marriage conferences where speakers said, "You know what my wife thinks is sexy? Vacuuming. If I vacuum, she's all over me like a hyena." Then all the husbands go home and vacuum. When their wives are unresponsive, husbands become more frustrated because their system of creating indebtedness didn't work.

Likewise, women are told that if they do certain things for their husbands, they will get the husbands they want. There is literally a book out there dedicated to changing your husband's behavior rather than you developing holistically as a couple. When the principles fail to deliver an improved husband, it just leads to more frustration.

My criticism of this kind of "best practices" stuff is that it doesn't address the heart. It doesn't use the Bible's only means of getting below the surface of behavior modification. It's always predicated on the idea that we are the ones who need our spouses to measure up to our standards, not that we have our own lack of measuring up to deal with.

The Scriptures show husbands that they've been called by God to love their wives like Christ loved the church. That means we love them regardless of their response to our efforts to change them. And the same grace-centeredness is needed for the wives who want their husbands to change.

Getting our hearts into this way of thinking is the hardest thing in marriage by far because all of us tend to love in order to get something in return. (You can tell when it's not really love you're giving if you begin to withhold it because you don't think the response is good enough.) Jesus calls us to a more selfless way, the way of the cross. His way calls us to love purely because it's the right thing to do, because it honors him and glorifies his Father. Jesus emptied himself in order to love imperfect responders. That's real love.

Men, have you figured out that you cannot be romantic enough? You cannot be sweet enough. You cannot help out around the house enough. You cannot make enough money and buy enough stuff to make your wife a sexual dynamo in the bedroom. Heart change isn't brought about through leverage like that. In the end, only the Holy Spirit can change your wife's heart. So we love, we encourage, and repeatedly we turn our wife over to Christ because he can change her heart. He can move in her. He can do things that we can't.

The same is true for women. You can give all the sex that your man wants. You can cook him all his favorite meals. You can keep the house extra clean. You can give him time alone in his man cave or whatever. And God can use all those things, but none of them performed to bring about change will work to change your man's heart. Only God can do that.

That is what happened with Solomon and his queen. Her heart was transformed and stirred up toward her husband when just a little while ago it wasn't at all. She was indifferent because she was tired. But then she became sick with love. God did that. Now notice the resulting appraisal: "My beloved is radiant and ruddy, distinguished among ten thousand" (v. 10).

This was a woman who twenty minutes before was saying, "Don't touch me. I'm not in the mood." Now she's going on about how hot he is:

> His head is the finest gold;
> > his locks are wavy,
> > black as a raven.
> His eyes are like doves
> > beside streams of water,
> bathed in milk,
> > sitting beside a full pool.
> His cheeks are like beds of spices,
> > mounds of sweet-smelling herbs.

His lips are lilies,
  dripping liquid myrrh.
His arms are rods of gold,
  set with jewels.
His body is polished ivory,
  bedecked with sapphires.
His legs are alabaster columns,
  set on bases of gold.
His appearance is like Lebanon,
  choice as the cedars.
His mouth is most sweet,
  and he is altogether desirable.
This is my beloved and this is my friend,
  O daughters of Jerusalem.
    (vv. 11–16)

Something definitely changed. She went from "I've got a headache" to "I want your body." Something shifted in her heart. And it wasn't Solomon who brought it about, because he wasn't even there. No, God moved. God worked in the deep parts of her heart. God restirred her affections for her husband. The Lord prompted her toward love, and she responded. He readied both of them to work toward resolution and reconciliation.

Look at the start of the sixth chapter: "Where has your beloved gone, O most beautiful among women? Where has your beloved turned, that we may seek him with you?" (6:1). Somehow the queen figured out where Solomon went: "My beloved has gone down to his garden to the beds of spices, to graze in the gardens and to gather lilies. I am my beloved's and my beloved is mine; he grazes among the lilies" (vv. 2–3).

He went to the garden. If I had to guess, I think he was probably wrestling with his frustration. He probably knew his frustration wasn't valid. So he sat alone, working through, processing, and praying.

This is a fairly typical male trait. Wives, you may think that in times of conflict, your husband is "shutting down," and this means he's not as engaged, not as invested in the relationship as you. Men tend to process things a little differently than women, though. Women tend to be more verbal in their processing, able to access multiple thoughts and feelings simultaneously and express them fairly quickly. Men need a little more stewing.

Women, if your man isn't talking straightaway, it doesn't necessarily mean he's not thinking about you and the problem and working through it. Men tend to process more internally. It's likely that Solomon was doing just that. He didn't want to react in a poor way, so he gave her a sign that he loved her and then stole away for a bit to be alone and work through his frustrations.

Getting away from the conflict can be an unhealthy thing if it's simply about avoidance. You can't ignore problems away. The conflict will still be there. Sometimes, it may be healthy to take a break, catch your breath, and process outside the heat of an argument or the immediacy of the frustration. And it's always good to get alone with God, to ask him to help you see what you ought to see about yourself and help you give the grace to your spouse that you ought to give. Not because he or she deserves it, of course, but because it is needed. And because God deserves it.

TALKING WELL

Solomon's wife found him in the garden. After they each had time to process their frustrations and feelings about the other, and they experienced a working of God in their hearts and minds, they were ready to work through their conflict in a healthy way. They may still have had the fight ahead of them, but they were prepared to fight fair.

My first few years of marriage were full of soul-shriveling conflict. One of the ways God led me out of that conflict (or maybe into it in a way that led to health and healing) was through the teachings of Tommy Nelson on this very chapter of the Song. Here are some "nevers" I learned from the principles of conflict that Tommy laid out in his books and sermons. These are not "best practices" in the sense that if you put them into practice, you are guaranteed positive responses. They are instead "gospel practices"—ways to show grace in how you talk through conflict with your spouse. These "nevers" have less to do with getting something from your spouse and more to do with what is the right way to speak to him or her regardless of his or her response.

Here are ten "nevers" of communication, especially as it pertains to conflict:[1]

1. Never respond to your mate rashly.

This has a lot do with thoughtfulness and maturity in responding, especially to charges or accusations. It is about moving from reaction mode to responding mode. Lashing out in anger is a sign of a lack of self-control. There will be times when you need to just take a deep breath when something stings you, lest you say something back that's completely irrational and hurtful. Maybe you need to count to ten or find another way to think and process before responding, but never speak rashly. Proverbs 29:11 says, "A fool gives full vent to his spirit, but a wise man quietly holds it back." Slow down, breathe, and think through what you're saying. Never speak rashly.

2. Never touch your mate out of temper or frustration, ever.

There are no ifs, ands, or buts to this. Physical abuse of any kind— even a slap—is totally off-limits always, forever, end of story. If you find yourself struggling with this, you should see a trained counselor without delay.

3. Never seek to shame your spouse in public (or in private for that matter).

This sin is as huge as it is common. Have you ever been at a table when this happened? Doesn't it create a stifling spirit of awkwardness? Never publicly embarrass your mate. It's obviously a handy way to humiliate her, to "put her in her place," but it's so damaging to the soul. The humiliation and the shame don't dissipate easily, if ever. Public shaming also wins you no allies; most people in these settings tend to immediately sympathize with the humiliated person. So if you want to kill the mood of a social engagement, shame your spouse, and lose friends, go right ahead and embarrass your spouse.

But if you want to do the right thing, hold your tongue. The desire to criticize and knock your spouse down to size in the presence of others comes from hell.

4. Never fight in front of your kids (or use them as leverage in a disagreement).

I come from a home that had some massive issues, so I've had a lot to work through. But by God's grace, in seventeen years of being with Lauren, we've never yelled at each other. Oh, we've had plenty of those "Don't ever do that again" kind of moments—an unbelievable amount of those. But we don't scream at each other.

This is extra important in moments when we're together as a family and some kind of conflict arises between Lauren and me. It usually takes place in the car and has something to do with getting lost. My wife has an uncanny sense of direction. She's like a human GPS device. Me? I am what the experts call "directionally challenged." And people who give me directions often make me mad because they'll say things such as, "Go east on 35." And I'm thinking, *Go east? Do I have a compass? Am I Davy Crockett?* Seriously. Why not say, "Take a left"? That's easy.

Getting lost is one of my most frustrating experiences. Sometimes we'll all be in the car, I won't know where I'm going, and Lauren will make fun of me or laugh at my poor sense of direction. I get irritated. I may become sarcastic in response. And our kids know. They know I shouldn't talk to Mom like that. It's an important lesson for all of us. They are learning from Lauren and me how mature and healthy couples handle conflict. And if we're always yelling at each other, losing our tempers, freaking out about unmet expectations, guess what they think is normal?

I promise you this: You are teaching your children how to fight. In your home right now, you are teaching your daughters how to treat their husbands and you are teaching your sons how to treat their wives. They're soaking it all up. They're taking from your home their expectation of "normal family life."

Be careful how you handle conflict in front of your kids. And never use them in any way to win an argument.

5. Never mention your spouse's parents or any other family member.

This is the part of a fight when things can get really crazy. Because, as I said, we bring our ideas of normalcy into our home lives with our spouses. And we end up with a lot of expectations that cause us to do a lot of measuring.

In my house growing up, you might just put your dirty towel on the floor, and Mom would eventually come by and pick it up. Pretty sweet deal. Then she washed and folded it and put it back in the cabinet. When I married Lauren, I left my towels lying around. I thought that was normal. And she would be like, "Are you serious?"

I came from a family background with one set of routines and expectations, and Lauren came from another. I expected her to adjust to my expectations, not really thinking that I ought to adjust to hers, because in her mind, it wasn't really about the towel but about respect.

If married couples don't handle these differences in expectations well, conflicts can become all-out assaults on entire families! Like,

"Your family is a bunch of idiotic cavemen to live that way!" Or, "Your family is a bunch of uptight neat freaks to live that way!" It can turn into a barrage of insults on each other's families, which is extremely destructive.

It happens in conflicts when you tell your wife she is just like her mother, when that is not a good thing to be. Or when you blame your husband's flaws on his parents' failure to bring him up right. These are very sensitive places to jab, and we typically jab there when we really want to hurt our spouses. So don't do that.

Keep the issue *on the issue*. You don't need to bring anyone else into the equation.

6. Never dig up the past; try to stay on topic.

Similar to the problem with bringing up somebody's family or upbringing is this issue of going back over past wrongs and failings. First Corinthians 13:5 says that love "keeps no record of wrongs" (NIV). It has been my experience in marriage, though, that sometimes love jots some stuff down on a napkin. There may not be an official ledger of offenses, but there's a mental list. It's brought out at key times, especially in the middle of conflict. So the argument stops being about just that argument and starts becoming about *all the things*.

The first two years of marriage for Lauren and me were very difficult. I thought she was a hypocrite in some areas of her life, and she thought I was a hypocrite in some areas of my life. And, really, who isn't? But we were both clueless and thought ourselves to be pretty holy, pretty put together. One of the things Lauren used to feel was that I didn't listen very well.

She would say, "When I'm trying tell you what I think the Lord's doing in my heart, I feel like you're not listening to me." I would be honest with her and say, "You know, I'm really not. I do kind of tune you out. It's hard for me to hear some of these things because I know the issues we have, I know what we're trying to work through, and honestly I feel like you're hypocritical at times." That was one of our issues early on.

Years later—and I remember the day—we were sitting out on our back porch, drinking coffee, and she was talking me through the book she was reading called *The Wounded Heart*. She told me how it was ministering to her and resonating with her. I was listening, but it was such a beautiful fall morning—birds chirping, sun shining, the scent of coffee in the air—that I sort of half listened and half took in the atmosphere. She picked up that I wasn't totally paying attention.

Later she went to get her hair done, and when she came home, I could tell she was upset with me. The conflict was brewing. I was thinking, *What did I do? I hung up my towel and everything. Why is she mad?* I had no idea. But as we were talking about this thing and it became more tense, Lauren said, "Do you still feel like I'm a hypocrite and that I'm not honest and open with you?"

I said, "What are you talking about?"

She said, "I was trying to tell you about what I was reading in this book and what the Lord was teaching me, and I just felt like you weren't even there. So you still think I'm a hypocrite about these things?"

And then I knew what she was talking about. I said, "Baby, you can't pull a file from six years ago!"

She was still smarting from my hurtful words that long ago and was bringing them up again. And I didn't feel that way about her at all. I didn't think that. But by withholding my focus from her that morning, I had brought that stuff back up for her, and so she brought it back up with me.

Sometimes we make a conflict deeper than it ought to be when we get historical. We may have said we forgave our spouses, but the proof that we actually haven't is when we start going back through the record of wrongs, listing them as ammunition against our spouses in any current conflict. And usually the reason we do that is because it gives us power in the argument. The more charges we can file, the greater our case. But thinking that way makes conflict not about resolution but retribution. And this leads us to our next principle:

7. Never try to win.

I had a counselor tell me in premarital counseling, "Do you want to be right, or do you want to be happy?" Two months into marriage, I found the fatal flaw in his reasoning. What if being right makes me happy?

For a lot of people, what makes them happy is being right, winning, no matter the emotional cost to their spouse. They want their spouse humiliated, whipped, chastised, properly penitent. It's so easy to slip into winning mode, and you can usually tell you're there if you've moved from responding to reacting.

In too many marital conflicts, we work too hard at winning the argument and too little at winning the heart. You can express your feelings and thoughts, even share criticisms and complaints, but the end goal of marital conflict should be care for your spouse's soul, not trying to rack up the most points. Seeking to win is not love.

8. Never yell, use put-downs, or verbally defame your spouse.

These sins are connected to the sin of rashness mentioned earlier. The Bible reminds us over and over about the devastating power of the tongue. Here is one example: "So also the tongue is a small member, yet it boasts of great things. How great a forest is set ablaze by such a small fire!" (James 3:5).

Women tend to be more vocal; they're very relational, so words are unbelievably powerful to them. You can hurt a woman with words very easily, often without even trying. When you couple harsh words with a raised voice or put-downs and insults, the wounds you create in your wife may last the rest of her life. Read that last phrase again: *the wounds ... may last the rest of her life.*

It's true for men too. I've never sat down with a guy who, if I pushed and prodded and tried to find it, couldn't tell me something harsh that was said to him when he was an adolescent, something that every once in a while comes back up and haunts him.

Words are powerful, and the way we say them—tone, volume, posture—only adds to their destructive strength. The childhood taunt "Sticks and stones may break my bones, but words can never harm me" is garbage. The damage that yelling and demeaning can do endures long after the conflict in which it occurred. Lore Ferguson wrote:

> I grew up in a home with a good amount of yell-
> ing. Excuses for it were common, as well as prefaces
> or follow-ups. What I learned early on is there are

levels of yelling, there is also tone of voice, there is not enough coffee, too much Irish in our bloodline, and too short a fuse. I learned yelling was the expected response and apologies came later, if at all. And I learned, most of all, that what is yelling *to me*, was not the universal decibel level of yelling.

Everyone has their own barometer of what constitutes yelling and when it is appropriate.

Because I'm a sinner and we're not in the new earth yet, I still find myself sensitive to the tones of voices around me, to how words are phrased and flung, and what excuses are given for anger. I am rarely offended, but if you yell at me, I'll be looking for the nearest closet. Fear of man is alive and well in this soul on this issue....

The longer it's been since I lived in a home with yelling, the more I realize yelling or raising your voice in anger is not functional, not ever. If you are a parent, there is no excuse for yelling at your child. Ever. If you are a child, there is no excuse for yelling at your parent. Ever. If you are a friend, you should never yell at another friend.[2]

And if you are married, you should never yell at your spouse in anger. Ever.

I know that seems really difficult for some of you to do. You were not raised in an environment where anger was handled in more healthy ways. Yelling seems normal. Or maybe it feels like part of your personality. You see yourself as passionate, emotional, and fiery. Raising your voice comes naturally.

But it's never right. The right thing to do in conflict is not "what comes naturally" but what God would have us do according to his Word. The right thing to do is to put aside the "natural" man and put on the Spirit.

9. Never withhold physical intimacy or use sex to manipulate.

Let's be honest: I think this is almost 95 percent of the time a wife's issue. I don't know that I've ever even heard of a relationship where the husband withheld sex to get his wife to act a certain way. I'm sure it's happened, but I've never heard of it.

Most of the time, this manipulative tactic is employed by a wife, in sort of a carrot-and-stick arrangement. It's fine for sex to feel like a "treat." But it's not fine to withhold the treats to get your spouse to surrender in conflict. It's a sinful way to resolve an argument, to be sure.

10. Never put off seeking resolution.

This comes right out of Ephesians 4:26, but it needs some explanation.

I'm not naive about the nature of some conflict, and I know that there are going to be some nights where you can't solve everything before bedtime. But there is something you can do to work toward peace in the meantime.

The day grows long, the evening sets in, and the conflict is still there. It doesn't look solvable. But as much as you are able, as soon as you are able, make an effort to take at least part of the responsibility for the conflict, no matter how small that part may be. Likely you're in the conflict because you think you're in the right. You both think that. So what can you do to own part of it? You're still convinced your spouse needs to own the lion's share, but you can take some of it, right?

Try to bring some semblance of peace to the home before you go to sleep. Extend an olive branch of some kind. If you don't do this and decide to go to bed sour, the Devil has a larger playground in your home, and overnight, the root of bitterness sets in deeper.

Let's say your spouse is 99.9 percent to blame for the conflict. (I know, most of you are thinking, *I don't have any problem imagining that.*) Let's say she did something wrong and didn't even apologize for it. But you blew up about it. You yelled; you compared her to her mother; you got out the laundry list of her past sins. She messed up, and it's her fault. But you responded poorly. Now you're both lying in bed. You're facing those walls, backs to each other. It's eerily quiet and cold in the room.

What if you decided to roll over, tap her on the shoulder, and say, "Honey, I apologize for blowing up." It's a great way to show grace, especially if you think you're the one who's been the most wronged.

This is critical to all healthy conflict in marriage—refusing to shift the blame and accepting whatever responsibility you can. It is the way of the gospel.

Paul Tripp said, "[Y]our biggest problem is not the imperfection of your spouse."[3]

No, the biggest problem in most of our marriages is *us.* And really, the only person we can control is us. We can't change our spouses. (Have you figured that out yet?) Only God can do that. So the only thoughts, actions, and words we can control are our own. Let's ask ourselves, then, what we can do to take responsibility in the midst of conflict. By owning our part, we can stop the escalation of conflict.

Don't let the sun go down on your anger.

LISTENING WELL

Now that we've covered some principles of talking well during conflict, I want to share principles with you for listening well. These are things to pray for more discipline in because the flesh's impulse will be to spring back into defensiveness and accusation in the midst of an argument. But love *listens*, and here are seven ways how:

1. Show that you are listening with your nonverbals.

Don't have your back turned; don't look all over the room; don't roll your eyes. Look at your spouse. Look him in the eyes. Show him with your face that you're paying attention and focusing.

2. Don't use logic to overpower feelings.

Here's what happens: A woman will say, "I just feel like, I just feel like, I just feel like …" and the man immediately starts thinking of all the reasons why she is not supposed to feel that way. He doesn't even wait for her to finish speaking; he just looks at her mouth, thinking, *Here's why you're wrong.*

So now she feels disrespected and not heard to add to her other feelings.

3. Don't debate.

It's hard not to argue when you're in an argument, of course, but one internal fight you can wage with yourself is learning what to respond to and what not to. When your spouse is saying particularly hurtful, invalid, or just angry, vindictive things, it's all right sometimes not to respond. I don't mean employ the silent treatment. You should talk. But don't feel the need to respond to every single point. Don't treat it like a debate. Don't argue. I think there are times when you have to let it go even if what's being said is wrong. For the sake of forgiveness, sometimes you may want to ask yourself, as Paul did, "Why not rather suffer wrong?" (1 Cor. 6:7).

4. Don't interrupt.

This should make obvious sense. If you're interrupting, you're not listening. Don't listen only to be listening for an opportunity to jump in. Listen to actually *listen*, and this means adopting a spirit of patience.

5. Don't leave prematurely.

This one is tough. We've seen in our biblical text that Solomon walked away. I would say there are certainly times when it's all right to take a break, to get some space and process and pray. Sometimes if a conflict is escalating too quickly and the venom is flying and it doesn't look like anything productive is going to come out of it, the best thing to do is take a breather.

But in the middle of conflict, when someone is sharing his heart with you, one of the worst things you can do is walk out. It shows a disinterest in the relationship. Walking out on someone who is pouring out his feelings—especially feelings of hurt—is akin to slapping him in the face.

You will need discernment in knowing when taking a time-out is appropriate and when it would be counterproductive, but abruptly getting up and walking out on somebody as she's talking is almost never the right thing to do.

6. Don't speak negatively or complain about your spouse to your friends.

This is similar to our point about not embarrassing your spouse publicly. She may not be in the room, but in a way that's worse because she isn't there to defend herself or give her side. This is a selfish ploy to amass supporters against your spouse; when in marital conflict, the healthy action is seeking to win the support of your spouse.

It's all right to seek counsel and advice from a trusted Christian friend, but this is obviously not the same thing as complaining. I think if you do talk to a friend about your conflict with your spouse, you should focus on which parts of the conflict you can own.

7. Avoid uninviting or distant body language.

Posture, position, gestures: all of these and more communicate whether we're receiving what is being said and considering it, or whether we are already closed off against it, planning to defend and deflect.

FORGIVING

Let's return to our text now and see how Solomon and his wife worked toward resolution and reconciliation.

The queen found her king in the garden. Things were tender between them. She had a change of heart, but there was probably still residual tension because they hadn't talked it out yet. And taking the conversational initiative, like a godly husband, this is what Solomon led with:

> You are beautiful as Tirzah, my love,
>> lovely as Jerusalem,
>> awesome as an army with banners.
> Turn away your eyes from me,
>> for they overwhelm me—
> Your hair is like a flock of goats
>> leaping down the slopes of Gilead.
> Your teeth are like a flock of ewes
>> that have come up from the washing;
> all of them bear twins;
>> not one among them has lost its young.
> Your cheeks are like halves of a pomegranate
>> behind your veil.
> There are sixty queens and eighty concubines,
>> and virgins without number.
> My dove, my perfect one, is the only one,
>> the only one of her mother,
>> pure to her who bore her.

The young women saw her and called her blessed;
    the queens and concubines also, and they
        praised her.

"Who is this who looks down like the dawn,
    beautiful as the moon, bright as the sun,
        awesome as an army with banners?" (6:4–10)

Solomon had plenty of time to think and process and pray for God's help. His wife found him in the garden, and while she might have been bracing herself for a real blast of anger and frustration, God worked in both of their hearts. Solomon didn't let her have it. Instead, he praised her in the joy and pleasure of their newlywed bliss.

You can tell that in the middle of all this conflict, real forgiveness happened.

Now consider her response in verses 11 and 12:

I went down to the nut orchard
    to look at the blossoms of the valley,
to see whether the vines had budded,
    whether the pomegranates were in bloom.
Before I was aware, my desire set me
    among the chariots of my kinsman, a prince.

And Solomon came back again with a reference to dancing.

Here's the primary thing I want you to see: Not only was forgiveness exchanged between them, but they met each other in the embrace of reconciliation, which restirred the romance between them. They didn't reach a stalemate or an uneasy peace. They really forgave each other. They set their grievances aside. Their conflict was handed up to heaven, not swept under the rug. And all the sorrow, shame, difficulty, and pain they both endured turned into dancing.

Conflict is going to be one of those things that define what happens in our marriages. There's no way around it. But how we handle it will reveal our own sin and our own insecurity more than anything else. It will be sanctifying.

You know, for a long time I felt really suckered into this Christianity thing. Because the message I heard was that Jesus loved me, and if I'd come to him, he'd fill me with joy. But nobody told me the second I gave my life to him, he would start tilling up the very deep places of my heart, revealing the darkest, nastiest things. Nor was I told about the stuff that would come to the surface so that I could deal with it and find my way to joy, through the cross. No one really preached that message.

I didn't know that God disciplines all those he calls sons and that he scourges those he loves. No one ever pointed me to Psalm 51:8: "Let the bones that you have broken rejoice." God crushes bones? No one ever showed me the end of Moses's story where God took him up on the mountain and showed him the Promised Land and said, "You don't get to go in. I'm going to kill you up here on the mountain." Never heard that one in Sunday school.

Likewise, Christian marriage gets elevated to this worldly notion of a struggle-free, conflict-free, happily-ever-after fairy tale because, you know, *we love Jesus*. But that's absurd. And unbiblical. And then Christians get married and go skipping naively into their lives together, and the 18-wheeler runs over them. And then they don't even feel like they can tell anybody that an 18-wheeler rolled over them, because they're supposed to be happy and problem-free with Jesus.

But that's not how God wants marriage to work in this fallen world. No, he uses marriage to take two sinners into places of deeper honesty with each other and deeper trust of him. Marriage is going to dig up some really dark things in people's hearts.

Walking according to the Spirit, though, we can learn to love each other well, take responsibility for our sins, and forgive as we've been forgiven. We learn to serve and sacrifice and submit in such a way that marriage becomes the real, deep, lasting joy it is meant to be as it glorifies Jesus Christ.

CHAPTER SEVEN

LOGS ON THE FIRE

My wife loves a fire in the fireplace. And it better not be one of those little gas things where you flip the switch and the fire comes on in that fake wood. She wants to hear the sap sizzling, the wood crackling; there needs to be legitimate danger of the house burning down. And it doesn't necessarily need to be overly cold for us to have a fire in the fireplace.

Because of this, every year there is a sort of two-month window of tension in our relationship because she wants a fire, and I'm saying, "It's seventy-two degrees outside; it's not time for a fire."

She'll say something like, "Well, it was sixty-four when we woke up this morning," as though that has any bearing on anything, to which I'll try to put my foot down. "We still don't need a fire. You're literally asking me to start a fire and also turn on the air conditioner."

And then we meet in the middle somewhere, which means I start a fire in the fireplace.

Therefore, we have a wood-burning fireplace that about four months out of the year is constantly burning. We used to be able to start the fire with gas, but we ran it so much one year that the pipe the gas came out of literally melted and broke off, so I could no longer light the fire the easy way. I had to actually go out and gather kindling and build the fire. What once was pretty easy to start became harder and harder.

Then we started getting ice storms, so I'd gather a bunch of extra wood and put it on our porch so I wouldn't have to go traipsing around when an ice storm hit. But what I didn't think through was that the fire I started when I left for work in the morning would still be going when I came home and all that wood I'd put on the porch would be used up. So now it's dark, freezing cold, and I'm wandering around in the ice looking for dry kindling.

I think relationships are a lot like this. For nearly all of us, the heat and the excitement of things in the beginning of marriage are fairly easy because attraction in and of itself produces zeal and gladness and excitement and a kind of nervous energy. But then, over time, the routine of knowing one another and the pace of life take a lot of that heat away. And that fire that was so easy to start in the beginning becomes harder and harder to get going.

Where there was once a roaring inferno, creativity, discipline, and pursuit, now, all of a sudden under the weight of life, the fire has died down somewhat. Maybe it's a nice little glowing fire, and that can be good. You can work with that. But maybe it's smoldering now, and there's barely any heat left in it.

It's in that season people begin to say things that are not indicative of having entered a covenantal union. It's then that couples often begin thinking the dying fire is a lost cause. It's not giving off any heat or light, so they assume they should wander off elsewhere to look.

But for the Christian who understands the marriage relationship as a covenant based on the grace of God in the gospel, we recognize that we do not "fall out of love" with our spouses, because love is not based on how we feel. It's based on the covenant itself, on the promises we made. Remember, marriage is not a contractual arrangement. True love doesn't say, "Make me feel this way if you want me to stay." That's not love. Instead, true love says in commitment, "I'm giving myself to you *regardless*."

Yet that fire still may look weak. Anxiety, fear, and weariness take their toll the longer a couple is together. Sometimes it has a lot to do with biology. Bodies change; metabolisms change; hormones change. Kids introduced to the home always change the dynamic. People change jobs, homes, cities. A marriage is constantly changing day by day based on the growth (or lack thereof) of the couple and on shifting circumstances around them. All of those little foxes get into the vineyard and start eating away at everything.

These stressors can dampen the fire, cut off the oxygen to it. If we're not careful, they can dampen and cut off the heat of our love for one another.

But if we're mindful, our fire doesn't have to go out. It may rage or flicker, but it won't go out, so long as we keep tending to it. You just have to keep putting logs on the fire. And maybe you've got to be out in the darkness, wandering around blindly in an ice storm to find them, but the work will be worth it.

As we press further into the Song of Solomon, we will learn valuable lessons about throwing logs on the fire of romance in our marriage.

PAY ATTENTION

Picking up in Song of Solomon 7, notice something different about the king's appraisal of his wife's beauty:

> How beautiful are your feet in sandals,
> O noble daughter!
> Your rounded thighs are like jewels,
> the work of a master hand.
> Your navel is a rounded bowl
> that never lacks mixed wine.
> Your belly is a heap of wheat,
> encircled with lilies. (vv. 1–2)

Did you catch it?

Every other time Solomon talked about his wife's body, he began with her eyes. But not this time. He mentioned her feet, her thighs, and then her stomach. There is a significance here we should not pass over lightly.

We should see Solomon and his wife as older now. They've been together for a while. Solomon was learning to see his wife in different ways that only he could see. No one knew what the queen's thighs looked like except for Solomon. The only one who looked upon and rejoiced in her belly was the king. In the privilege of marriage, this man got to know this woman like nobody else, and vice versa.

Husbands and wives, one of the gifts that God has given to us in marriage is this treasure hunt of finding things in our spouses that nobody else can (or should). What a gift to be given by God, to spend decades with someone, Lord willing, in a safe covenant relationship, where you can know these intricate intimacies that no one else gets to see.

There are things about Lauren that only I know. I believe there are times that even Lauren doesn't know. They are things that only I get to see, aspects of her that are amazing and beautiful that come with the honor of being one flesh with her.

And the way I get to take advantage of this gift is to bring those things to her attention. Sometimes we'll sit down and talk about our goals, where we're trying to go together, whether or not we're on track, how we want to handle the kids, that kind of thing, and those are some of the times I say to her, "Hey, I've seen this in you. I just think it is so amazing." And she'll look at me, surprised and pleased at the same time. I can see it's a blessing to her.

If you want to throw logs on the fire of romance, husbands and wives, here's the first thing you have to do: *pay attention*.

You have the opportunity to see things that no one else does. So pay attention, study your spouse, learn him or her, and then you can turn around and use the things you've learned to demonstrate your love.

I met a guy named Dudley Collison years ago, and he told me the story of how he got engaged. It blew me away. He started by picking up his girlfriend in his car and driving out to a lake. At the lake, they got into a canoe and canoed out to a little island in the middle of the lake. There in the middle of the lake, Dudley had set up lunch. They ate a sweet, romantic meal together. After lunch, a speedboat came flying up to the island to pick them up, so they got in the speedboat and sped around the lake for a little while before going back to shore, where there was a limo waiting for them. They got in, and the driver took them out to an airfield, where they boarded a little plane and went flying over the beautiful hills of Arkansas. When they landed on a little grassy runway, they were at a nice college campus in the area. He led her out of the plane and to the campus chapel, where the whole thing was set up as if for a wedding. Candles were lit, flowers sprinkled everywhere. She saw an envelope up front with her name on it, so she went to open it, and inside was his proposal for marriage. She turned around, and Dudley was down on one knee with the ring out.

Of course she said yes. Next, he escorted her to a waiting truck— a really beat-up piece of trash that barely ran. But they got in and drove to dinner, where he explained what all the vehicles meant.

He said the car stood for normalcy, for the reality that they were going to have mostly normal days in their life together. The canoe was for the times they would have to work together to get some- where. And the speedboat was for the fun they were going to have. The limo represented other people driving them, anticipating times when their lives would be affected by other people. The airplane was about their spiritual journey together. Finally, the old, beat-up truck was about growing old together.

And that's how this guy proposed to his wife.

But there's more. The two of them got married on the thirty-first day of the month. Dudley figured out that there are seven months with thirty-one days each year, and on every one of those thirty-firsts, he buys a small present for his wife and places it somewhere for her to find. It's always something she likes, things he's been taking notes on all the other days. So she might get into her car on the thirty-first day of a month, turn it on, and a new CD just starts playing. It's a nice surprise.

He says that after fifteen years of marriage, on the thirty-firsts, his wife wakes up and just starts looking!

I met this guy when I was a college student, and I thought, *Teach me, Jedi master.*

Most of us need a little help with this stuff, right?

We can be honest and say that Dudley's example may be a little extreme. But we can learn a lot from him about paying attention to our wives and using what we see to bless our wives' hearts.

Most men throw all the weight of their romance into three holidays: their wife's birthday, their anniversary, and Valentine's Day. And that's pretty pathetic, guys. You're better than that.

Start paying attention to your wife, and start turning what you learn about her into intentional blessings for her. Pick a couple of dates a year to do something really creative, something really out of the ordinary. Use Google if you need help with ideas. Check out Justin Buzzard's book *Date Your Wife.* There are lots of resources out there.

If you are paying attention, your wife will tell you what she likes and doesn't like without you asking. You know those days when somehow you've agreed to go to the mall with her, and you're in that Bataan Death March through the stores? Well, if you stop sulking, you'll hear her say things like, "Oh, that's cute," or "I love that," or "I hate this kind of thing." Pay attention to that. Take notes, literally if you must. Put it in your cell phone.

Pay attention when she comments on things in magazines or books or in television commercials. Pay attention at restaurants when she comments on different food and drinks. Don't just consider it chitchat. Consider it research.

Then you can turn your notes into presents and surprises later. Or maybe just in conversation you'll be able to bring up her likes and dislikes. She will notice that you've paid attention, and that will bless her. A woman desperately wants to be known. You may have even heard your wife say from time to time, "I don't feel like you really know me." This is a big deal for her. Food and drinks and clothes may seem small in the grand scheme of things, but your remembering her little likes and dislikes is a way to show you are listening, paying attention, and remembering. They are ways to throw logs on the fire.

Bring home flowers for no particular reason. Send her texts and emails telling her you're thinking about her.

But let's not forget that men want to be desired and pursued too! Solomon's wife tore off after him when he was gone, and that must have been a huge blessing to him. He went for a walk, and she didn't think, *Fine, then, go; I don't care.* She went after him.

I earnestly believe that, biblically speaking, husbands should be the primary pursuer in the relationship, but wives bear responsibility to tend to their husbands in some initiating ways too.

Wives, there are two big ways you can do this that will bless your husbands tremendously. The first is with words of encouragement and respect. Build him up. He deals every day with criticism—internal and external. If your husband is like most men, he is haunted by feelings of inadequacy and failure, and he will nearly always struggle with insecurity about his masculinity, his strengths, and his gifts. You are in an extraordinary position to either add to these insecurities or combat them, and *your words mean the most to him*. Aside from the voice of God in his Word, yours is the most powerful voice influencing your husband's heart.

Pay attention to the things that wound or heal your husband, and intentionally speak words that do the latter. Become a student of his likes and interests. Become an expert on his strengths, not simply a noticer of his weaknesses.

The other important thing to do is flirt with your husband. Show initiation with affection and sex.

Paying attention to one another, becoming students of each other, is an important way for a married couple to weave romance into the fabric of their relationship. It's a big log for the fire.

GET AWAY

Sometimes you have to take a break from the routine.

Vacations are great. If you have the means to go out of town or get away from the kids at a hotel or even just a long date, take advantage of that.

For many, however, the finances don't allow a lot of date nights or trips away, so you will have to be more creative about carving out time in your lives to get away together. You can learn to redeem the time together, no matter how much time or money you've got.

Some of my favorite moments with Lauren are early in the morning before the kids get up. We sit together on the back porch, read our Bibles, drink coffee, and enjoy the quiet of the morning. We don't always even need to talk in those moments, but we're together, enjoying the small pleasures of life, and it's a very sweet time. Many times it's a great opportunity to catch up, hear each other, and share our hearts. It's like a little getaway to start the day.

When we have a date night out, we oftentimes add things on the back end of the evening to make sure we don't get home before the kids are in bed. We try to redeem every little bit of time we have— whether it's over lunch breaks, date nights out, chilling out after the kids are in bed at night, or our early morning coffee.

Try to pull out of all the craziness that's going on in your life and make sure you focus just on one another in those times. Because if you don't, you increase the likelihood of taking the stress out on each other.

You've got to do what you can to make some time to be with each other, focused and relaxed and enjoying one another. That is exactly what Solomon's wife said to her husband:

> Come, my beloved,
>> let us go out into the fields
>> and lodge in the villages;
> let us go out early to the vineyards
>> and see whether the vines have budded,
> whether the grape blossoms have opened
>> and the pomegranates are in bloom.
> There I will give you my love.
> The mandrakes give forth fragrance,
>> and beside our doors are all choice fruits,
> new as well as old,
>> which I have laid up for you, O my beloved.
> (7:11–13)

"Let's go on vacation," she said. "Let's get away."

And if you read well between the poetic lines here, she was being extremely erotic and flirty about it in 7:13, when she basically said, "I've got all those old fruits you enjoy so much. And I've got some new stuff to show you too."

You think that, hearing that, he's not going to move some meetings around? I'm guessing after she said that, his schedule cleared pretty quickly.

On our anniversary and a couple of other times a year, I ask some questions of Lauren, things like the following:

What am I doing well?

What do I need to get better at?

How can I help you?

If you ask your spouse these questions, you have to ask with a listening heart and a patient spirit. You can't ask with a ready defense waiting. If you're truly interested in increasing the fire in your marriage, you have to boldly ask for your spouse's appraisal and carefully consider it, holding fast to what is true (see 1 Thess. 5:21).

This is one of those areas in our relationship that I've had to grow in because for a while I was really terrible at it. If Lauren expressed feeling a certain way or gave me even a little criticism, no matter how valid, I was quick to explain why her feelings were invalid and her appraisal was wrong. I never acknowledged that her feelings were legitimate.

So it took awhile to get Lauren to trust me enough to say, "Yeah, I think you could do this better. I think this would be more helpful in this area," without fearing that I was going to go on the attack or get defensive or explain away her thoughts.

Responding correctly is very hard to do at six thirty at night when I've just walked in the front door from work and there are three screaming kids running around and dinner in the works, right? That's not the time for this kind of conversation. But if we can get away for a bit, we can have it in a relaxed, open setting.

Do what you can to get away. It is a log on the fire.

WORK HARD

That firewood didn't appear on my porch magically. Even though it was dark and freezing cold, I knew my baby wanted a fire in that fireplace, and if I was going to provide it for her, I was going to have to do some work.

I think probably the greatest enemy of keeping the fire burning in our marriages is just plain laziness.

We must constantly guard against the tendency to downshift into tepid relational dynamics. I don't believe that the fires of passion can always be at honeymoon level, but all of us in marriage are called by God to tend the fire. We have to watch it, keep an eye on it. When it gets low, we're responsible to throw more wood on the fire.

If you're in a place where that fire's gone, where the whole room just seems dark and cold, remember that Christians are covenant people. We have committed ourselves to one another.

Remembering this, we confess, we repent, and we seek forgiveness from our spouse, and we begin to figure out how to get that flame going again. I think marriage counseling would be a huge help for many couples, but so many won't go because they think it's just for couples on the verge of divorce. Or they won't go talk to their elders or pastor or a counselor at their church because it seems too embarrassing or inconvenient. Favoring the deadness of a marriage over the embarrassment or inconvenience of breathing life back into it is just plain lazy.

Some great questions you can ask your spouse are as follows:

"How can our marriage get stronger?"

"How can I love you and serve you more effectively?"

"What is it that makes you feel loved, valued, and desired?"

Then with great discipline, seek to win, woo, nurture, serve, and make much of your spouse. He or she is God's gift to you, and you waste the gift of marriage if you don't actively tend to it. Don't give up on the fire.

I think the only way you have a shot at marital intimacy on a deep level is to survive years five and six. Too many marriages in our country don't survive into their seventh year. Or even if the marriage is intact, the relationship is not. It consists of two people sharing a bed and maybe a checkbook, but little else.

Solomon and his queen worked hard at their marriage. Time passed, the years added wrinkles and pounds, but they still complimented each other, still flirted with each other, still pursued each other. They were intentional.

Romance is a discipline. You can't be lazy and expect romance to blossom in your marriage.

DELIGHT IN EACH OTHER

This is a hard truth to consider, but it is not optional for a husband and wife to find joy in each other. I know joy doesn't always come

naturally to us. We either like something or we don't; either we are
pleased by something or we aren't. But part of working hard and
learning our spouse is finding joy in him or her. And because our
spouses are made in the image of God, because they are equipped
with gifts and strengths and talents—and especially because we made
a commitment to them to love in good times and bad—there are
ways to delight in them. This is the way of Christ, who rejoices over
us (see Zeph. 3:17).

Gary Thomas called rehearsing dissatisfaction in marriage a sin,
and he wrote:

> Whenever marital dissatisfaction rears its head in
> my marriage—as it does in virtually every mar-
> riage—I simply check my focus. The times that I
> am happiest and most fulfilled in my marriage are
> the times when I am intent on drawing meaning
> and fulfillment from becoming a better husband
> rather than from demanding a "better" wife.
>
> If you're a Christian, the reality is that, bibli-
> cally speaking, you can't swap your spouse for
> someone else. But you can change yourself. And
> that change can bring the fulfillment that you mis-
> takenly believe is found only by changing partners.
> In one sense, it's comical: Yes, we need a changed
> partner, but the partner that needs to change is not
> our spouse, it's *us*!
>
> *I don't know why this works.* I don't know how
> you can be unsatisfied maritally, and then offer

yourself to God to bring about change in your life
and suddenly find yourself more satisfied with the
same spouse. I don't know why this works, only
that it does work. It takes time, and by time I
mean maybe years. But if your heart is driven by
the desire to draw near to Jesus, you find joy by
becoming like Jesus. You'll *never* find joy by doing
something that offends Jesus—such as instigating a
divorce or an affair.[1]

The dissatisfaction comes so easily, but then we put the work
into justifying our lack of delight. According to God's grace in the
gospel, however, we ought to be fighting against our dissatisfaction,
working harder at what John Piper calls "the duty of delight." Look
hard into your spouse; there is beauty there, charm and wonder. You
can find delight, maybe even that original delight of the early days,
if you will look hard enough through the lens of grace. Shirley Rice
wrote to wives:

Are you in love with your husband? Not, Do you
love him? I know you do. He has been around
a long time, and you're used to him. He is the
father of your children. But are you in love with
him? How long has it been since your heart really
squeezed when you looked at him?... Why is it
you have forgotten the things that attracted you to
him at first?... By the grace of God, I want you
to start changing your thought pattern. Tomorrow

morning, get your eyes off the toaster or the baby
bottles long enough to LOOK at him. Don't you
see the way his coat fits his shoulders? Look at his
hands. Do you remember when just to look at his
strong hands made your heart lift? Well, LOOK at
him and remember. Then loose your tongue and
tell him you love him.[2]

As you get older as a married couple, as things change, the things
you take delight in may need to change too. Or you may need to
change your approach.

In Song of Solomon 7, we see that our couple has grown older
together and done much of life together. They've put a lot of hard
work in. And they've reaped some tremendous romantic benefit
from it. How do we know? Well, he talked about her body, how he
continued to find her sexy as all get-out, and she said, "We work
pretty smoothly together now, don't we?"

What happened? The awkwardness was gone. They knew where all
the buttons were, so to speak, and they knew how to press them. That's
not something you get in the first year of marriage; it takes time. It takes
years. It takes a lot of hard work, a lot of study, and a lot of grace.

We have this image of young married sex as the great sex,
but that's such a false notion, really. If you keep the fires burning
throughout your marriage, it only gets better. You get better at it, for
one thing. But you also learn each other's bodies; you have the fruit
of all your labors.

And this is true for much more than just sex. Couples who get
through those difficult seasons, weather the conflicts, work toward

peace through God's gospel, and endure to the end find that their later years are so unbelievably sweet and rich. The difficulties make them that way, like all the pressure that turns coal into a diamond.

You may envision an old couple fumbling around with each other's buttons and think, *Ew*. But it is beautiful. It is the fruit of all their hard work.

Solomon and his wife tumble like a couple of randy newlyweds into chapter 8:

> Oh that you were like a brother to me
> who nursed at my mother's breasts!
> If I found you outside, I would kiss you,
> and none would despise me.
> I would lead you and bring you
> into the house of my mother—
> she who used to teach me.
> I would give you spiced wine to drink,
> the juice of my pomegranate.
> His left hand is under my head,
> and his right hand embraces me!
> I adjure you, O daughters of Jerusalem,
> that you not stir up or awaken love
> until it pleases. (vv. 1–4)

At the end of it all, she looked back on their journey and said, "We did it the right way." She had a sense of satisfaction, a depth, a gratitude that culminated in this joyous proclamation: "We didn't arouse love until it was time, and the result has been a love incomparable, a love unquenchable." All the hard work, the conflict, the romance, the wrinkles, and the extra weight—they were all worth it.

This is the sweetest fruit, the kind that comes from a long romance.

You can start now, today. You don't have to give up because you've wasted time. Just stop wasting time. If Christ is in your marriage, the fire of marriage can be stoked again. Pay attention, carve out time for each other, work hard, and delight fully.

CHAPTER EIGHT

"I'M NOT GOING ANYWHERE"

Song of Solomon chapter 8 is probably the most difficult of the chapters in the book. It sets a vision for us of a life well lived, a picture of that final season when we can look back and almost hear in our ears the Savior saying from the finish line, "Well done, good and faithful servant."

From our earthly perspective, life seems long and difficult. Assuming we live that long, what will it take to get to the days of great age and smile in deep satisfaction?

I have had for quite some time a vision of how I would like my life to look when I am eighty years old. Maybe I won't get that far, but I still have this mental picture. I'm sitting on the back porch with my wife, drinking our coffee, and I'm hanging out with my friends Bleaker and Doug and Josh and Bryan. We're reflecting back on our ministry life together and just marveling at what God has done through a group of morons like us. We tell story after story of his faithfulness. "Do you remember when God did that? Do you remember how he rescued us that time? Do you remember when he did that amazing thing?"

And then I get to play with my grandbabies. I get to watch them run and play and sing and dance, and my wrinkly face is just smiling.

Then, with whatever strength I have left, I get up to go and preach.

I look forward to preaching in my eighties because you can get away with stuff that you simply cannot get away with when you're in your thirties or forties. When you're in your thirties and forties, people are always like, "We ought to talk to him about that." When you're in your eighties, people are just like, "Well, you know, he's eighty." I figure that if I get to that point, having served faithfully for so long, I'll be afforded some crazy.

All kidding aside, I just want to get there. I have in my head and in my heart a great desire to reach those moments. I want to get to the point where my war, if you will, is over, and although I'm still in the fight, there are younger, stronger guys on the front lines whom I can applaud and encourage and build up.

Now, I have learned in the last few years that the likelihood of me getting to eighty is not so great. I've had a significant succession of clean scans after my battle with brain cancer, but it's not so likely I will get to my eighties. But I know the God whom I serve. I'll trust him with my days, knowing nothing ever surprises him. I'm not even promised tomorrow. It doesn't have to be cancer that takes me out.

Yet the thought of finishing well still drives me. I just want to get to the end of my race. If that's in two years from a brain tumor or in a car wreck next week or at peace in my sleep when I'm eighty-five, I want to run my race well. I want to get to the end and know that as best as I could, by the grace of God, I gave myself to him. I want to be able to say that I tried to lie low, exalt Christ, and walk in humility.

I want my life to speak a humility that says, "Christ is the ultimate treasure. Christ is the one who should be exalted. Christ should be the one you applaud and love. And I did nothing but what he asked of me."

That's how I want to finish up.

And I hold this vision out before me, illuminated by the light of my seventeen years with Lauren, praying for many more. I am not perfect. I won't fulfill this vision perfectly. All the time, I find so much new sin in me of which I need to repent. When I look back, I see so much I regret, some sins long repented of that still haunt me today. But I know that God is faithful and that he will get the glory.

From what we know from the context of the greater biblical story line, Solomon's story eventually took a turn toward some really sinful stupidity. But that does not negate the wisdom he has for us. There is still much to learn from him in this inspired Word of God. We trust that the Holy Spirit worked through this man, and I trust that the Holy Spirit will work through me.

So this is what we see in our last chapter together: how we can finish well. And the first thing to remember in setting a vision for finishing life well is that even as you slow down in so many ways, you don't stop moving forward.

STILL PURSUING

Let's revisit Song of Solomon 8:1–3 and get that glimpse back into the romantic life of Solomon and his wife:

> Oh that you were like a brother to me
>> who nursed at my mother's breasts!
> If I found you outside, I would kiss you,
>> and none would despise me.
> I would lead you and bring you
>> into the house of my mother—
>> she who used to teach me.
> I would give you spiced wine to drink,
>> the juice of my pomegranate.
> His left hand is under my head,
>> and his right hand embraces me!

One of the things we see in our aged couple, despite all their history together and familiarity with each other, is that they still pursued one another. Looking over these few verses, we see things like the following:

> "I find you."
> "I kiss you."
> "I lead you."
> "I bring you."

They may have moved more slowly, but their love didn't slow. They staunchly refused to give into becoming civil roommates.

Notice, too, how they demonstrated their love, first in public (in the streets) and then in private (in the house). Their love was not a show. They didn't hold hands in public to keep up appearances and then go cold behind closed doors. Neither did they reserve all their affection for the private moments.

Whenever you see an elderly couple out at the park or in a restaurant together, and they're tender with each other, holding hands or talking sweetly, aren't you moved by that? Maybe he opens the door for her or helps her out of the car. Maybe she wipes food off his chin or helps him order because he can't see or hear very well. They are affectionate with each other in a sweet way, so that you see how in sync they are, how the rhythms of their life have led to this great romantic togetherness in their old age. That's very moving.

The human soul is a deep thing, and in different seasons the heart will manifest in different ways.

Regardless of our life stage, regardless of where we are in our marriage, there's still a pursuit. Don't let your mind in this moment drift to autopilot. Don't think, *Well, I'll worry about that when I'm in my eighties.*

No, this is how you *get* to your eighties. This is how you invest in that beautiful future. Keep pursuing. Don't stop.

Continue to pursue your spouse's heart. Continue to press the gospel into his or her spirit. Continue to want more.

When you get there, you may be ready for retirement from so many things, but you should never retire from romancing your spouse. Don't work toward the day to quit. Work toward the day you die.

This is how true longevity occurs. We will never arrive at a place where we can say, "I know you now," because it simply wouldn't be true. Each day we are called to know and pursue our spouse more deeply.

STILL STAYING

Now we move forward in the Song:

> Set me as a seal upon your heart,
>> as a seal upon your arm,
> for love is strong as death,
>> jealousy is fierce as the grave.
> Its flashes are flashes of fire,
>> the very flame of the LORD.
> Many waters cannot quench love,
>> neither can floods drown it.
> If a man offered for love
>> all the wealth of his house,
>> he would be utterly despised. (vv. 6–7)

For the record, the word for "love" in this passage is that word *ahava*. It's the clinging love, the "I'm not going anywhere" love.

Ahava is as strong as death. Its flashes are fiery, sourced in the consuming fire that is God. All the oceans covering the earth cannot drown *ahava*. It is worth more than all the treasures of the world.

If we're going to be faithful to the end, we will often have to lean into the covenant that we made with our spouse and with the Lord. We will need to access again and again, by God's grace, this devoted *ahava*, which says, "It's not an option for me to go anywhere because Jesus would not abandon his bride."

I have been physically fit my entire life. I am tall and lean and have always been strong for a man as lean as I am. I have been told I have a powerful presence. I like to have fun, I like to goof around, and I have been blessed with what seems to be a boundless amount of energy. These were things that attracted Lauren to me. She often described me as our family's "recreation coordinator."

But then I got sick.

And all of that strength and vitality, in a matter of months, simply vanished. The ability to be playful, the ability to be creative, the ability to goof off were gone. Not only that, but my ability to really take care of myself, to do fairly simple tasks, vanished. I couldn't even take a shower by myself, and the kind of accompaniment I needed there was not sexy, all right? I lost the ability to even stand.

I lost so much of my ability to, in a way, *be myself.* There was no way I could romance my wife. My desire for sexual intimacy was gone. For a while I began to wonder what the brain surgeries had done to me. I wondered if, should I ever get over this cancer stuff, I would always be unable to do some of the things I enjoyed so much. Maybe I was going to be broken this way for a long time.

Lauren saw me at my worst. I wasn't in that kind of depressive "I hate everyone" mentality, but I was at my worst in terms of being very weak, unattractive, unstable, unable to get myself to the toilet so I could vomit and lie on the cool tile of the floor. I was a mess. And in those moments, I praised God for *ahava* love. As I look back, I still praise God for *ahava* love.

I praise God that this flighty kind of Cupidian, Valentine-y, emotive love isn't what we're hoping will hold us all together! Praise God that the love we trust to keep us from falling apart is *ahava*. Praise God that as miserable and messy as I was, my wife was a regular reminder of God's grace to me. She didn't turn and run. She stayed with me, helping me, loving me, and carrying me. Lauren demonstrated her love toward me in this: that she lived into an *ahava* love even when I could not reciprocate.

///

The first seven years of our marriage were very difficult. My heart grew dark on multiple occasions. I remember one occasion in particular because it marked a real turn in our marriage. I had said some very cruel things to Lauren that day. I was frustrated; I was angry. I thought she was selfish and self-absorbed, and I told her so. I admit with shame that I *wanted* to wound her.

I was in the kitchen, and she was around the corner, sitting in a chair in the other room. I was being a terrible person, just hateful, and I threw some words out there that I knew would cut deep. I didn't even regret that I said them; I wanted to hurt her.

This venom came out of my mouth, and I was fuming. I'm not a yeller, but as some of you probably know, I do have a pretty loud voice, so I don't often even need to yell. I just put the words out there and hoped they really stung. I was in that kitchen acting like a big baby, clanging dishes around.

I'll never forget this: Lauren came around the corner. I was steeling myself for whatever she'd throw back at me and getting ready to fight back. But she just came up and grabbed me. Then she pulled me really close to her, and she began sobbing. She cried and cried and cried as she held me. She said, "I don't know what happened to you, but I'm not going anywhere."

Those were maybe the most powerful words I'd heard up to that point in our relationship. I was at my absolute worst, and she had every earthly reason to say, "Forget this. Forget you. I'm done." But she didn't.

"I'm not going anywhere."

Can you believe that?

It broke me. It wounded me in the good way, in the right way. It startled me and helped me in a way I could never foresee or imagine.

"I'm not going anywhere," she said.

And that's when I said, "I'm going to get help."

Do you see? That's *ahava*. That kind of love isn't "Oh, he's strong. He's funny. I love the way he does this or that." That kind of love is "This is awful and it hurts a lot, but God is good and God is mighty, and by his power, I will endure and give grace."

Ahava is faithful to the end because Christians are a people who lean into the covenant of grace. We're people who say, "No, I won't bail. I've given myself for better or for worse to this person."

It doesn't mean we don't get help. It doesn't mean we stay in abusive situations. It just means we're faithful to the covenant we entered into with God and our spouse.

I think one of the bigger lies we tend to believe is that whomever we end up with is supposed to complete us. But the reality is, whomever you are married to is going to disappoint you. In fact, the person you're married to will likely be responsible for your deepest hurts.

Even in the best of marriages, there will be hardships to over-come. There will be difficult days. There will be frustrating behavioral patterns. There will be crises that expose parts of the heart you didn't know were there.

Solomon said, "Set me as a seal upon your heart." Seal it. And then he went on to talk about the "violence" of *ahava*. He wasn't talking about physical violence but a kind of resolute forcefulness, the same kind Jesus spoke of when he said, "The kingdom of heaven has suffered violence, and the violent take it by force" (Matt. 11:12). It's the kind of forcefulness that says, "You're not going to move me off this ground. You're not going to push me off this stance. I will love. Against all odds, weathering all storms, I will stay."

Here in Texas we get to enjoy a very weird sense of pride. The pride of place here is more than any state I've ever been in. It's a "We're bigger; we're better; we should be our own country; we would do it better than anyone else" kind of thing. For instance, as far as I can tell, no other state has a proliferation of bumper stickers that say, "I wasn't born here but got here as quick as I could." That's Texas.

Some of that is rooted in the legends and lore of our state. First of all, there have been six flags flying over the state of Texas. And I'm not talking about the amusement park. There have been six sover-eign nations that ruled over us. One of those flags was our own: the Republic of Texas. And here we are. We've survived, endured.

Laid deep in the ethos of all Texans is the Battle of the Alamo. What happened there? Well, a group of men hopelessly outnumbered stood their ground and said, "Bring it." Then they all died. I mean, that's how the story ends. Everybody died. But they held their ground. They dug their boots into the ground and said, "If you're going to take it, you're going to have to take my life. We will purchase for our brothers, for our sisters, the opportunity to live to fight another day, so I'm digging in my boots. And if you're going to try to get me out of here, you're going to have to kill me." So they did.

That's a picture of *ahava*. Digging in the boots. Standing your ground. Saying, "Bring it."

This is what you do on your wedding day. That's the vow you make. "Till death do us part."

Bring on the flood! Many waters will not quench *ahava*. It can't be flooded.

Bring on poverty! *Ahava* is better than all the riches in the world.

Bring on death! *Ahava* will never die.

Prepare yourself now to lean into that covenant. Be prepared for dark days, dark months, dark years. It's a broken world, and nobody gets out without bleeding. So in our minds and in our hearts, it's a wise thing to know this life is going to be difficult.

Now, what does that mean for abandonment? What does that mean for physical abuse? What does that mean for serial, unrepentant adultery? Well, I think those are some unique categories. The Bible addresses them in different ways. Obviously, if you've been abandoned, your option to stay has been removed. There's no one to stay with. Paul said, in so many words, that if this happens, you are free.[1]

If you are being physically abused, I would not counsel you to stay in the abuse. You should get out of that situation. Talk to the authorities; talk to your pastors; talk to your family. I don't think divorce is always the necessary option, but I would not advise anyone being physically abused to "stick it out." Bringing resolution and, if possible, repentance and restoration to such a toxic situation doesn't work like that. You should remove yourself from the environment, and if you need help doing that, you are absolutely within your rights to get it.

Given the "normal" sins of marriage, the messiness and the brokenness, as difficult and wearying as it can be, we must remember that the vows exist for precisely such experiences. You don't really need to make a vow to stick with someone in the best of times. The inclination to run doesn't exist then. It's the low times the covenant is made for.

Isn't this a reminder that grace exists for sin? We would not need grace if we weren't sinners.

As you plan for the future of your marriage, as you look forward to those twilight years, remember your vows to *ahava* so that in the darkest days, in the lowest moments, when all hope seems lost, you can say, "I'm not going anywhere," and when you've finally arrived, you can rejoice that you endured to the blissful end.

STILL BUILDING

Now let's read to the end of the Song and see where the attention turns in the couple's finishing of their race:

> We have a little sister,
> and she has no breasts.
> What shall we do for our sister
> on the day when she is spoken for?
> If she is a wall,
> we will build on her a battlement of silver,
> but if she is a door,

we will enclose her with boards of cedar.
> (vv. 8–9)

This was the chorus chiming in, saying basically, "Hey, we have a young daughter who hasn't gone through puberty. She is not a woman yet. What are we to do when a man comes her way?"

If she's a wall, they'll build armor on her so that a man can't get to her. If she's a door, they'll build cedar around her so that he will not be able to get to her.

Here's how the queen responded:

> I was a wall,
>> and my breasts were like towers;
> then I was in his eyes
>> as one who finds peace.

> Solomon had a vineyard at Baal-hamon;
>> he let out the vineyard to keepers;
>> each one was to bring for its fruit a thousand
>>> pieces of silver.
> My vineyard, my very own, is before me;
>> you, O Solomon, may have the thousand,
>> and the keepers of the fruit two hundred.
> (vv. 10–12)

Then Solomon rejoined the song: "O you who dwell in the gardens, with companions listening for your voice; let me hear it" (v. 13).

Here is the third key to staying together and finishing well in your marriage: looking not just to heaven ahead of you but to the legacy behind you.

Remember back in chapter 8, verse 4, we heard a repeat of the admonition not to "awaken love until it pleases." Why is that there? I mean, if they were growing old together, why would they worry about that? Hasn't the time to awaken love long since passed?

See, there's a slight twist in the Hebrew text there, and the queen was not saying, "Don't awaken love until it's time" to Solomon but to others, to the "daughters of Jerusalem." She was counseling others.

In verses 8–9, the subject of the younger generation comes up. What do you do with the young girls (and, we can assume, the young men)? Solomon and his wife had wisdom to share with the younger generation. Their ministry was not over; it only shifted some of its focus. They didn't retire their wisdom and coast. They kept building a foundation for the future, for the generations coming after them.

Suddenly all their mistakes and sins didn't seem wasted. They had lots of things to teach, and a lot of that teaching consisted of what *not* to do. This is one great way that God redeems our sins and our stupidity.

There is no experience of joy or loss that has not been redeemed by Christ and now is used by the Holy Spirit of God to minister to others. What tends to dominate people in their failures is a feeling of inadequacy, as though the loss can't be redeemed. That's wrong thinking. Every failure in your life, every shortcoming, every stumble, every bloody knee, every broken nose is redeemed by Christ and used by the Holy Spirit to help shape, mold, and serve what's behind you.

The Bible is very clear about how we are to engage those who are younger than us, whether in age or spiritually. Consider Titus 2:2–8:

> Older men are to be sober-minded, dignified, self-controlled, sound in faith, in love, and in steadfastness. Older women likewise are to be reverent in behavior, not slanderers or slaves to much wine. They are to teach what is good, and so train the young women to love their husbands and children, to be self-controlled, pure, working at home, kind, and submissive to their own husbands, that the word of God may not be reviled. Likewise, urge the younger men to be self-controlled. Show yourself in all respects to be a model of good works, and in your teaching show integrity, dignity, and sound speech that cannot be condemned, so that an opponent may be put to shame, having nothing evil to say about us.

The younger generation will praise us as examples of wisdom because we've invested in them, taught them, mentored them, and encouraged them. We built a legacy of faith and endurance for them to continue adding on to. We laid a strong foundation for the next generation of ministry.

When I came to pastor The Village Church, we were a church of about 160. I was twenty-eight years old. Lauren was pregnant with our first child. We very quickly hired a man named Gilbert Montez, an older guy who was an empty nester.

I praise God for that man because I felt so lost in so many ways. I had no idea how to do things. I had read all the books and researched all I could, but there's a time when research falls apart in the line of fire.

Then our daughter Audrey came into the world. We were losing sleep. When that's all you know, it's like, "Oh man, is this the rest of my life? Do I ever get to sleep again? Will I ever not be tired again? Will she ever be able to just tell me what she wants?"

Gilbert came alongside my wife and me and said, "It won't always be like this. This is a season. Be faithful in it. Enjoy it. It won't be here long." He spoke truth into our marriage and poured so much wisdom into me.

There have been older women who have come alongside my wife and mentored her and taught her so much.

I don't care if you're twenty-seven and your marriage is just coming out of a season you'd call a train wreck. As the Lord grows you, heals you, and begins to create a new relational dynamic between you and your spouse by his grace, your experiences are going to be invaluable. Your dark days will become jewels to pass on later in life.

For the first five or six years at The Village, we were so terribly young it was embarrassing. I just hated it. We were so hungry for gray hair.

We'd have all these twenty-year-olds sitting around, giving each other advice. It was like blind men describing vision to other blind men. We were making a bunch of mistakes, but we didn't know it. We were finding the land mines by stepping on them.

We didn't need a bunch of people coming in acting as though there was a way to never get blown up. We just needed people who'd stepped on a few land mines to come in and help us know what to look for. We needed people with some scars, with some wrinkles, with some white hair, with *some hard-won wisdom* to help us grow up. We needed people further along to help us get further along.

Don't let the Enemy make you feel as though your marital stumblings and failures have no redemption in them. In fact, let those failures and stumblings be redeemed by the Lord, and learn how to serve the Lord together in those shortcomings.

Lauren and I frequently meet with a couple now. Sometimes we just have dinner. I know all we're doing at that dinner is navigating their relational conflicts. They've been married for just a few years. Lauren and I are able to dig into our treasure chest of missteps and help them. We're not sitting around, thinking, *Gosh, I wish I could get those seven years back! Man, how could I ever talk about marriage now? How could I possibly stand up here and preach the things that I've preached when I've failed so miserably in so many of these areas?*

No, no. The cross bids me to share. The cross bids me to boast of my weaknesses.

The grace of God says, "Brother, you know better than most."

Who might compassionately walk alongside the alcoholic but one who's been delivered from alcoholism? Who's more qualified to encourage those struggling in marriage than those who may bear some scars but made it through?

One of the keys to longevity is serving the Lord together. Keep building; keep building; keep building.

One of my greatest joys in this season of my life—and I'm not an old man, I know, but I've been weathered a bit—is in how Lauren and I are able to minister so well together. Of course, there are things that I do alone and Lauren has things that she does alone, but we try as often as possible to overlap those things. We stay in tune with one another so she feels as much as possible a part of my ministry, and I do hers. We serve the Lord together. It's part of our marriage health.

As I pastor an ever-growing church and manage a growing ministry platform, she's very much in the trenches with me. The Lord has called *us* to this ministry, not me to this ministry.

We are building together. And by God's grace, year by year, we will keep building together, passing the baton as God calls younger and more energetic pastors and couples. And when our knees get creaky and our hands get shaky and our eyes grow dim, we plan to keep building as best we can, to leave the best legacy we can so the generation behind us has as much wisdom as possible.

STILL BELIEVING

I love how the Song of Songs ends. Look at this: "Make haste, my beloved, and be like a gazelle or a young stag on the mountains of spices" (8:14).

We conclude much as we began: with pursuit, desire, and hope. The Song started with the romantic hope of, "Let him kiss me with the kisses of his mouth!" (1:2) and ends with, "Keep leaping over those mountains! Get back to me! Keep pursuing me!"

What marks our relationships as men and women, husbands and wives, is the ongoing pursuit of one another for the glory of God and our eternal joy. Why? Because this is the way God designed it to work, and in God's good design, our joy and his glory are found.

Your need for a Savior will never be more apparent to you than when you're trying to faithfully walk in the wisdom laid out in the Song of Solomon. And so my earnest hope for you, for me, is that the Holy Spirit will sustain us with faithfulness until the end. May we fight against becoming just good roommates. May we lean hard into the covenant in difficult days. And may we see our shortcomings redeemed and as empowerment for us to mentor in strength and wisdom into the brokenness of others.

May we go year by year, serving the Lord together with gladness. And may our hearts and lives be marked by a legitimate pursuit of one another day in and day out. It will not be easy. We will get distracted. God has given us the tools of repentance, confession, and forgiveness. He has laid before us the methods of how to fight well. He has shown us how important it is to seek outside counsel. He has demonstrated to us how to respond to another seeking forgiveness.

Regardless of your stage in life, the first relationship I would spend a lot of time considering is your relationship with God. Read this closely, just so you're not thinking in some sort of ambiguous "Yeah, I love God" kind of way. What I'm talking about in your relationship with God is not that you're behaving a certain way but rather that you have surrendered your life to Jesus Christ.

Do you find your gladness ultimately in Christ? Only in him is ultimate gladness found.

Learn to find your rest in Christ alone. Learn to lean into him as your only strength and wisdom. If you don't, nothing else will make the forever kind of sense.

If you don't understand that Christ died for your sins, and if you don't know that you are loved, forgiven, and adopted, then you will miss out on the joy that no date, no wedding, no marriage could ever deliver.

It is the gospel and our belief in it that make dating, courtship, engagement, marriage, and growing old together unbelievably vibrant. It is our understanding that God just keeps forgiving us for the same things over and over and over again that informs our patience with our spouse. It is the unbelievable romancing of God toward us as the bride of Christ that should inform and motivate our romancing and pursuit of our spouse.

So first and foremost, we must consider Jesus. We must consider this great salvation offered to us in Christ.

It is possible to have a decent marriage outside of Jesus Christ. Our next-door neighbors for years were unbelievers, and they were kind of gross to watch. They were in their sixties, and they would be out in the garden and they'd pinch each other, and … I mean, it was just disturbing. I almost called the cops one time, like, "I shouldn't have to see this."

But here's what I found out about them: they loved one another and loved life and had grown children and grandbabies, and they were doing great. They had a great marriage, a marriage that in many ways could be emulated. But they will never have the spiritual mingling of souls. Because, although they might be able to come together physically, emotionally, and intellectually, they will never be able to connect at the deepest possible level, at the spiritual levels, where Christ's washing of his bride is made visible in the marriage of his saints.

It makes all the difference.

Although marriage is not eternal, you can eternally waste your marriage if it is not built on Christ.

Marriage, properly understood, is an understanding of the grace of God made manifest in the life, death, and resurrection of Jesus Christ. We see this gospel mystery gleaming in the beams of old covenant light in the Song of Solomon. I pray that you've had the eyes to see them.

May we be people who know God and love him. And may our knowledge and love for him lead us to ongoing repentance, confession, and the seeking out of healthy, vibrant, strong relationships. May we pursue one another often for the glory of his name and to reflect all the more the beauty of his romantic pursuit of us as his covenant people.

In love, dating, courtship, marriage, and sex—as in all things— *Christ is all.*

CONCLUSION

The Song of Solomon has been interpreted in a variety of ways over the last several millennia. It has been allegorized out of proportion on one extreme, turned into the bluntest of practical textbooks on the other. The truth of its resonance lies in neither extreme, but somewhere in the middle. In the Song we certainly learn many practical things about romance, marriage, and sex. The Bible is eminently practical, even in its poetry. While we cannot overspiritualize the Song, turning all of it into a metaphorical anthem bearing no resemblance to the very real marriage in its vision, we do see that beyond the practicality, beyond the history, beyond the earthiness of its subjects, it definitely points outward, upward, away from itself and to him for whom all songs of praise are due.

Woven into the complexity of Solomon's symbolic Song is the profoundest of mysteries, just like woven into the complexity of marriage itself is the profoundest of mysteries. Paul put it this way, borrowing from the Old Testament: "'Therefore a man shall leave his father and mother and hold fast to his wife, and the two shall become one flesh.' This mystery is profound, and I am saying that it refers to Christ and the church" (Eph. 5:31–32).

Anyone who has been married for a substantial length of time can confess that marriage is many times a mystery. We really don't know what we're doing. But what a great reassurance it is to know that God does! He knows exactly what he's doing.

The things that surprise us, that freak us out, that send us into emergency mode—they don't faze him at all. The triune God is never in an emergency. He's never freaked out, never surprised.

As we fumble around in the darkness, then, holding our spouse's hand, looking for the light, we will find it not in each other's eyes, not in the roaring fire of romantic bliss, but in the Savior who loves us and gave himself for us. When we can see that marriage is about more than marriage—certainly about more than a man and a woman individually—and about Christ's deep, sacrificial, eternal love for his bride, we will really, truly *see*.

One day our marriage will give way, either by death or by the Lord's return. In any event, our marriage was not built for eternity. But the sanctification our marriage will bring into our souls is. One day we will be presented to our Redeemer, like a bride adorned for her husband. Then, when we see face-to-face, we will understand what marriage was truly all about. Until then, we enjoy the mystery. It is an amazing gift, a profound grace.

Yes, we enjoy the mystery of marriage. And give all the glory to its beautiful Author.

NOTES

INTRODUCTION

1. Gen. 1:1.
2. John 10:10 NIV.
3. Gen. 2:18.
4. Song of Sol. 2:16.
5. Gen. 2:25.
6. Gen. 1:28.
7. Duane Garrett and Paul R. House, *Song of Songs/Lamentations*, vol. 23B of *Word Biblical Commentary*, ed. Bruce M. Metzger (Nashville, TN: Thomas Nelson, 2004), 25.
8. C. H. Spurgeon, *The Metropolitan Tabernacle Pulpit Sermons*, vol. 42 (London: Passmore & Alabaster, 1896), 285.

CHAPTER 1—ATTRACTION

1. *Psychology Dictionary Online*, s.v. "What Is Attraction?," http://psychologydictionary.org/attraction/.
2. Erica Reischer and Kathryn S. Koo, "The Body Beautiful: Symbolism and Agency in the Social World," *Annual Review of Anthropology* 33 (2004): 297–317.
3. See Emily Peng, "History of What Society Viewed as Women Beauty," *SlideShare*, May 18, 2011, www.slideshare.net/emilypeng1/history-of-what-society-viewed-as-women-beauty-8005550.
4. Reischer and Koo, "The Body Beautiful," 298.
5. For the sake of clarity, here are the specific textual notes from net.bible.org (https://net.bible.org/#!bible/Proverbs+31) pertaining to this passage: "*Heb* 'a woman of valor.' This is the same expression used to describe Ruth (e.g., Ruth 3:11). The term לַיִל (khayil) here means 'moral worth' (BDB 298 s.v.); cf. KJV 'a virtuous woman.' Elsewhere the term is used of physical valor in battle, e.g.,

'mighty man of valor,' the land-owning aristocrat who could champion the needs of his people in times of peace or war (e.g., Judg 6:12). Here the title indicates that the woman possesses all the virtues, honor, and strength to do the things that the poem will set forth."

6. Bill Hybels, *Who You Are When No One's Looking: Choosing Consistency, Resisting Compromise* (Downers Grove, IL: InterVarsity, 2010).

7. Anthony Gross, ed., *Lincoln's Own Stories* (New York: Harper and Brothers, 1912), 109.

8. Tim Keller, Twitter post, June 22, 2014, 9:00 a.m., https://twitter.com/timkellernyc /status/480742216718352384.

CHAPTER 2—DATING

1. Elizabeth L. Paul, Brian McManus, and Allison Hayes, "'Hookups': Characteristics and Correlates of College Students' Spontaneous and Anonymous Sexual Experiences," *The Journal of Sex Research* 37 (2000), 76.

2. Tracy A. Lambert, Arnold S. Kahn, and Kevin J. Apple, "Pluralistic Ignorance and Hooking Up," *The Journal of Sex Research* 40 (2003), 129–33.

3. Lambert, Kahn, and Apple, "Pluralistic Ignorance," 129–33.

4. Tommy Nelson, *The Book of Romance: What Solomon Says about Love, Sex, and Intimacy* (Nashville, TN: Thomas Nelson, 1998), 42.

CHAPTER 3—COURTSHIP: AN OLD IDEA REVIVED

1. Tommy Nelson, *The Book of Romance: What Solomon Says about Love, Sex, and Intimacy* (Nashville, TN: Thomas Nelson, 1998), 49.

2. Joshua Harris, *I Kissed Dating Goodbye* (Colorado Springs, CO: Multnomah, 2003), 188.

3. John Thomas, "What Role Do Parents Play in Courtship?," Boundless.org, July 31, 2006, www.boundless.org/advice/2006/what-role-do-parents-play -in-courtship.

CHAPTER 5—"AND THE TWO BECOME ONE FLESH"

1. H. D. M. Spence-Jones, ed, *Song of Solomon* (London; New York: Funk & Wagnalls, 1909), 93.

2. Gary and Betsy Ricucci, *Love That Lasts: Making a Magnificent Marriage* (Gaithersburg, MD: PDI Communications, 1993), 159.

3. C. S. Lewis, *The Screwtape Letters* (New York: Macmillan, 1951), 102.

4. Gary Thomas, *Sacred Marriage: What If God Designed Marriage to Make Us Holy More Than to Make Us Happy* (Grand Rapids, MI: Zondervan, 2000), 226.

5. Shaunti Feldhahn, *For Women Only: What You Need to Know about the Inner Lives of Men* (Sisters, OR: Multnomah, 2004), 93.

6. Feldhahn, *For Women Only*, 93–94.

CHAPTER 6—FIGHTING FAIR

1. The ten "nevers" of communication were adapted from Tommy Nelson, *The Book of Romance: What Solomon Says about Love, Sex, and Intimacy* (Nashville, TN: Thomas Nelson, 1998), 135–38.

2. Lore Ferguson, "Some Observations on Tone of Voice," *Sayable*, June 16, 2014, http://sayable.net/2014/06/some-observations-on-tone-of-voice/.

3. Paul David Tripp, *What Did You Expect? Redeeming the Realities of Marriage* (Wheaton, IL: Crossway, 2010), 120.

CHAPTER 7—LOGS ON THE FIRE

1. Gary Thomas, *Sacred Marriage: What If God Designed Marriage to Make Us Holy More Than to Make Us Happy* (Grand Rapids, MI: Zondervan, 2000), 101.

2. Shirley Rice, *Physical Unity in Marriage: A Woman's View* (Norfolk, VA: The Tabernacle Church of Norfolk, 1973), 3–4.

CHAPTER 8—"I'M NOT GOING ANYWHERE"

1. See 1 Cor. 7:10–13.

THE MINGLING OF SOULS
ULTIMATE SMALL GROUP STARTER KIT

Designed for couples, singles groups or church gatherings.

A walk through Song of Solomon in 12, 30-minute teaching sessions by Matt Chandler and exclusive and candid question and answer session with both Matt and Lauren Chandler.

Study Guide written and designed to make it easy for anyone to lead a group and create engaging conversation.

MATT CHANDLER

TO VIEW THE SERIES AND MORE INFO GO TO WWW.GOTOTHEHUB.COM

Matt Chandler on Philippians

Using Paul's radical letter to the Philippians as his road map, Matt Chandler forsakes the trendy to invite readers into an authentic Christian maturity.

The short book of Philippians is one of the most quoted in the Bible yet Paul wrote it not for popular sound bites, but to paint a picture of mature Christian faith. While many give their lives to Jesus, few then go on to live a life of truly vibrant faith.

Available in print and digital editions everywhere books are sold

JOIN THE CONVERSATION

Tell your friends, share quotes, ask questions, discuss the book, discover extra resources: **#MinglingOfSouls**

CONNECT WITH MATT CHANDLER

TheMinglingOfSouls.com

Twitter.com/MattChandler74 (MattChandler74)

David C Cook
transforming lives together

Photo courtesy of Jesse McKee